GRADUATION
DAY

GRADUATION DAY

The Best of America's Commencement Speeches

Edited by

Andrew Albanese and Brandon Trissler

With an Introduction by George Plimpton

William Morrow and Company, Inc. New York

Library of Congress Cataloging-in-Publication Data
Graduation day : the best of America's commencement speeches / with
an introduction by George Plimpton ; [compiled] by Andrew Albanese
and Brandon Trissler.
      p.   cm.
   ISBN 0-688-16033-6
   1. Speeches, addresses, etc., American.   2. Baccalaureate
addresses.   I. Albanese, Andrew.   II. Trissler, Brandon.
PS663.C74G73   1998
815'.01—dc21   97-53253
                                              CIP

Printed in the United States of America

First Edition

1   2   3   4   5   6   7   8   9   10

BOOK DESIGN BY BERNARD KLEIN

www.williammorrow.com

To our parents:
David and Sharon Albanese
and Dennis and Janice Trissler

Contents

III
REMEMBER THE PAST, EMBRACE THE FUTURE

IV
YOU WILL SUCCEED

V
A LOOK BACK

Introduction:
We Don't Want You Out Here

George Plimpton

The invitation to speak at a graduation ceremony usually arrives in midwinter. The occasion itself, months ahead, tends to put the speaker at ease. Plenty of time to invoke the muse. So the invitation is accepted ("I am very honored and look forward . . . ") and then filed away. Invariably, it is only a few weeks, if not days, before the event itself when the speaker in a state of panic reaches for *Bartlett's Familiar Quotations* and settles down to work. The pages are riffled. The more common words for a suitable quotation might include "Career," "Success," "Goals," "Wall Street," "Family Values" (not in my *Bartlett's*), "Groves of Academe," "Brevity," "Love," "Livelihood," "Advice," and so on. Sometimes the reference isn't especially helpful. As an experiment I've just looked up "Career" . . . to find that Sir Walter Scott's offering (from *The Lay of the Last Minstrel*), "His bright and brief career is o'er / And mute his tuneful strains," is not especially adaptable. On the other hand I've looked up "advice" . . . to find among the choices the Earl of Chesterfield's maxim: "Advice is seldom welcome; and those who want it the most always like it the least"—a splendid aside to drop into one's opening remarks.

Speaking of advice, I have looked through the speeches that follow to see what my fellow speakers have come up with. Here is a sampling: "Never lose faith," "Love one another," "Raise strong families," "Find out about your grandmother's grandfather," "Walk across the Brooklyn Bridge," "Make babies, lots of them, say twenty-five," "Lay off the television," "Make a chocolate cake," "Listen to your own drumming," "Play to win every point," "Get up every morning and say, 'The wonderful mind I have is a genetic gift,' " "Don't just sit there and look at a bell; ring it," "Kick ass," "Smell a flower," "Sleep in the nude," "Don't lose heart," "Don't play it safe," "Equip yourself with a baloney detection kit," "Believe in yourself," "Believe in America," "Turn up the heat," "Indulge the cool in you," "Find every ounce of the messy plutonium," "Lean against the wind," "Always keep the shower curtain inside the bathtub," "Unpack, go back to your room."

This last exhortation is mine, and it is interesting to note that if I had made it a couple of years earlier—during the student unrest during the late stages of the Vietnam War—I would have been hooted off the stage by students eager to get out of academe in order to save the world.

Whatever the timing, it strikes me that the above list is a handy thing to have around graduation. Some years ago I was speaking at my daughter's graduation from her school on the shores of Narragansett Bay. Halfway through my speech, the concluding pages were lifted off the podium in a gust of wind and swept away across the lawn. The students in the front row chased after them, plucking one page out of the air, trapping another underfoot, and eventually delivering what they had captured back to the podium. I can't recall exactly what I said in the interim—a somewhat helter-skelter pursuit after the main thrust of my remarks (very much like the students chasing down my speech). How helpful it would have been to have the above list available in my wallet, say, able to pull it out and read it very slowly, nodding in agreement at each piece of advice, while the students chased after my speech. The audience might have been puzzled by the Brooklyn Bridge reference, sleeping in the nude, and filling potholes with hot asphalt, but generally speaking the suggestions are pretty heady. . . .

The following remarks are from George Plimpton's 1977 speech as Class Day Speaker at Harvard University's commencement exercises. Mr. Plimpton is a graduate of Harvard.

I have been led to understand that tomorrow you are going to graduate. Well, my strong recommendation is that you don't go. Stop! Go on back to your rooms. Unpack! There's not much out here. Chekhov tells the story of the traveler faced with three roads . . . if he takes the one to the right, the wolves will eat him up, if he takes the one to the left he will eat up the wolves, and if he takes the one to the center he will eat himself up.

The point is we don't want you out here very much. We on the outside see graduation as a terrible event—the opening of an enormous dovecote from which spring into the air tens of thousands of graduates. What is particularly disturbing is that you all come out at the same time—June—hordes, with your dark graduation cloaks darkening the earth. Why is it that you can't be squeezed out one at a time, like peach pits, so that the society can absorb you without feeling suffocated?

My own profession is being swamped with writers coming out of college, despite the condition out here that no one reads. Indeed, my friend Kurt Vonnegut was saying the other day that the only solution to the moribund state of publishing would be to require of all those on welfare that before receiving their welfare checks, they must hand in a book report.

So go back to your rooms and stay. True, there may be some practical problems. The deans may come tapping at your door like hotel concierges wondering about check-out time. Tell the dean through the door that you don't think you should go out into the world with a C minus in Economics 10. Great damage can be caused to the economic structure, and probably already has, by Harvard men out there who earned a C minus in Economics 10; you must tell the dean you don't want to compound such a situation.

The dean will say that he needs the room for the junior who is going to become a senior—the process must go on. Tell him there's no reason why the juniors can't stay juniors, the sophomores, sophomores, and the freshmen, freshmen. Tell him to stop the process. Why *should* the process go on? The *Harvard Lampoon* has had, in its century of operation, one hundred different editorial boards. Has it improved? Probably not. Why not keep the same one?

Besides, we are told all the time what a marvelous institution Harvard is. Benjamin DeMott once likened Harvard to the continent of Europe: "Either you've been there or you haven't." And you'll all remember the Boston dowager who said of a nephew: "He doesn't go to college, he goes to Brown." Why do they tell us such things if they don't want us to stay? So tell the dean you're convinced. You've decided to stay. You're not going to budge!

After a while the dean will go away. Deans always go

away. They go away to ponder things. They will assume that your parents will finally force the issue. They'll want you home. But I am not so sure. I have the sense that parents would rather not know what's being sent home to them these days from the colleges—not unlike receiving a mysterious package tied with hemp, addressed in rather queasy lettering from Dutch Guiana.

They'd much rather you stay here. When a mother is asked about her son at the country-club dance she can always say: "Why, John's off at Harvard." There's something quite grand about that certainly compared to: "Well, the last time I saw him he was . . . throwing a frisbee in the backyard."

If your parents insist you pack up and come home, there are always measures. If you're a chemistry major, tell them that you've become very attached to something in a vat of formaldehyde. If you're in pre-law, tell them that you're thinking of bringing home a tort. Your parents will probably have forgotten what a tort is, if they ever knew, and it *sounds* unpleasant—something that your mom wouldn't want to have stepping suddenly out of a hall closet. Surely, there is hardly an academic field of one's choice which does not have a nightmare possibility with which to force one's parent to pony up enough to allow nearly a decade of contemplation in one's room.

You'll remember the King in Alice in Wonderland. When asked: "Where shall I begin?" the King says, "Begin at the beginning, and go on until you come to the end; then stop." What I am suggesting is that you stop at the beginning, stop at your commencement. It's not very interesting to stop at the end—I mean *everyone* does that. So stop now. Tell them you won't go. Go back to your rooms. Unpack!

GRADUATION
DAY

I

Make the World a Better Place

You hold all of our futures in your hands. So you better make it good.

—JODIE FOSTER

Jodie Foster

Yale University
May 23, 1993

*Jodie Foster is one of America's most talented and successful
actresses. In 1988 she won Academy Awards for Best Actress
for her work in* The Silence of the Lambs *and* The Accused.
*She returned to her alma mater, Yale University, to deliver
this commencement address, which is full of humor, wit, and
intelligence. Few speakers have ever captured the essence of the
college experience as well as Foster does in this brilliant
speech.*

This is an extraordinary feeling for me to be standing up here
today and looking at this sea of faces framed by these incredible imposing buildings and filled with nostalgia. You
have to understand that this is a dream for me to be here
again. This place has meant so much to me and my life. But
don't worry, I'm not going to make the mistake of waxing
drearily about the Yale of the good old days like some horrible alumni bore in a beaver coat, weeping loudly into one
of those big old "Y" co-op hankies: "Ah, for my youth again,
for God, for country, and for Yale!" No, that's not me. I was
born in the seventies; that's not my style. I also hope to spare
you the kind of pompous intellectual rambling generally as-
sociated with these events—no obscure Greek poets, no
long-winded treatises peppered with incomprehensible foreign-
syllable words and a yen for the nasal. Not my way.

I also will not stoop (well, maybe a little bit), but I will
not stoop to entertain you with insensitive jokes about the

coed experience or finely tuned bathroom humor like my 1984 graduation speaker did—he'll remain unnamed, thank you.*

So what's left? More to the point, what exactly do I have to say to you on the eve of such a great, sublime, and terrifying moment in your life? And why have I been chosen to comment on the end of something so personal and so unique to you and to your experience? I mean, do I fit the bill of a Yale alumnus like George Bush or William Buckley? Huh? I'm not even ten years older than you, and I belong to the entertainment industry, better known in the press these days as "the devil." You know, that source of evil, liberal elite bent on moral pollution—that's me. I'm a feminist, a humanist, and I like very, very spicy, spicy food. And I don't even wince and apologize when I tell you that. Regretfully I'm not much for Yale Club functions or social events that require leaving the house for more than a couple of hours. Aside from the fact that I've enjoyed a certain amount of success to help color the alumni magazine, what could possibly be this traditional Yale link that binds us together like some secret handshake or some Flintstone moose call? Or to quote Bill Cosby, my favorite person to quote, "Who made me sheriff of the Jell-O today?"

I'm not quite sure, but I guess I'm going to plod ahead before everybody wakes up and kicks me off the podium. I suspect that this is an example of the typical Yale impostor identity syndrome. I'm sure you've all become familiar with that by now. It's the one where you hear the clock ticking and you wait for some kind of stewardess to tap you on the shoulder and say, "I'm sorry. We've made a terrible mistake in the records department. I'm afraid you're an idiot; you don't know what you're talking about. Kindly remove the

---

*On second thought, let's name him. Jodie Foster and Yale University's class of 1984 were regaled by the bathroom humor of Dick Cavett.

potato chips from your mouth, and follow me to the dungeon." Wait, wait, wait, am I the only one who ever thought that? How embarrassing? This is terrible!

But as long as I've decided to bare all of my insecurities here today, let me be perfectly honest. I don't remember a single fact I learned here. I don't remember a single date, or quotation or abstruse reference, but I do remember this: I remember singing at the top of my lungs with my arms around a bunch of friends, wobbling down that street right over there, High Street, laughing and singing and vowing the loyalty of the truly inspired and intoxicated. I still pledge allegiance to that particular flag, although I can't remember anything of that night.

I remember another day leaving the most stimulating and enlightening seminar that I ever heard, running down those steps, of Wright Hall, seeing my friends, who were sitting on the lawn wearing black, lying all over each other. My heart was racing, and my head was pounding, and I was so excited that I couldn't sit down. I just kept stammering and giggling uncontrollably, looking earnest and frightened at the same time. I guess I just had what's called a "perfect moment," to quote Spaulding Gray. That's one of those moments when the head and the heart and the spirit kind of come together in one place inside you. I can vaguely remember it having to do with the Oedipus myth or some such thing, but I can't remember the facts. And no matter how silly and ephemeral my epiphany may seem now, the moment itself was huge. It was extraordinary and monstrous. I told my friends what I was feeling that day, and they actually didn't laugh. They threw me down on the lawn and hugged me like a big, dumb, slobbering dog, and we were all big, dumb dogs at heart, and none of us had learned to be ashamed of it yet.

I remember crying my guts out, feeling that extraordinary pain and longing at the loss of my first love, seeing the walls move all by themselves, watching my feet step slowly beneath me, entirely detached from will. They were like zombies in a sci-fi movie, and it all felt much too painful to live through and too awful to finally realize that you are in fact alone in the world, no matter how often you deceive yourself to the contrary.

And of course I remember the assassination attempt on President Reagan, which occurred my freshman year*—an enormously impactful event on my life, not to mention on the life of James Brady, then press secretary of the United States and survivor of that shooting, and also an avid champion of gun control. The awful events aside, I remember the bursting of my privacy and the end of my Yale anonymity, or rather, the end of the illusion I had been carrying of it. I also remember three words that I repeated over and over again and that I'll forever carry into my conscious life and work: "Too much fear." And I suppose that I lost control for one of the very first times in my life right over there [Foster points to the College Street side of Old Campus]. A valuable lesson in survival. No matter how far down you fall, you can get back up somehow.

I remember all of those "eureka" moments brought about by love, pleasure, tragedy, dancing, snowstorms, loud music, drugs, surrender, and abandon. The big questions: What is pleasure, what is pain, what is trust, what is authentic, what is merely convention? What is a completely ridiculous lie? Who are my parents? Where do they stop and where do I begin? Who are my lovers? Where do they stop and where do I begin? Who are my mentors, my family and my enemies? Where do I stop and where do they begin? What is

---

*On March 30, 1981, President Ronald Reagan and his press secretary, James Brady, were shot outside the Washington Hilton Hotel by John Hinckley, Jr. Hinckley said he committed the act to capture the affections of Jodie Foster, with whom he was psychotically obsessed.

certainty? What is deception, how do I feel, in here, in here and out here? [Foster points to her heart, her head, and around her body.] This is beginning to sound a little bit like the game show *Jeopardy!*—"I'll take 'What is the College Experience?' for one hundred dollars."

The point of all this dribble is, well, I believe this place is a magical place, this often haunting and haunted place. This is a place of the "I." We're characters revealed as fate, to borrow from Heraclitus.* This is the place where I learned to love this life, to curse this life, and to claim this life for my very own. And as foolish and romantic and painfully intellectual as this may seem on this beautiful spring day in this most revered historic hall of learning, there is nothing in this world that I am prouder of than my ability to feel, to survive, and yes, to be a fool for what I love and believe in.

And I'll even venture foolishly enough to say to you today that every tangible piece of worth, every notch on my proverbial belt—from Oscars to professional respect to fulfillment to comfort and self-knowledge—stem directly from this center, from these lessons in the "I" that I taught myself right here. And for each and every one of you, that journey's been and will be different. Your respective "I"s have been challenged and prodded by the different ideas, peoples, and experiences you experienced around here. But do I believe that the goal will be the same for all of you?

How does the "I" get better instead of worse? How does it reveal its character more fully as opposed to settling for an approximate shape? How does the "I" leave its mark on the world as proof of having existed? And in my case, those questions came immediately after graduation, after I spent my requisite six months of depression, lying in bed for fourteen hours a day, not wanting to ask the next big question I

*Heraclitus, Greek poet and philosopher, c. 540–c. 480 B.C.

couldn't answer, like "What the hell am I doing lying in bed all day?" And somewhere between a lot of naps and some late-night reruns, I found something to get very passionate about: my work. I often say that in my life there are only three things: love, work, and family. And I've been lucky to occasionally find all three in my job.

So let me tell you what I do for a living (I include all my various professions in this analogy). I put all my stuff—my history, my beliefs, my experiences, my passions, and taboos and personal foibles, my weaknesses and unconscious agendas and eccentricities—I put them delicately and precisely on the tip of the proverbial arrow. I take careful aim, keep the target in my sight, and try desperately to communicate all that is me in a straight line toward an audience. But I am only human. My eyesight is faulty; my hands are shaky; a million things will distort the goal. And no matter how well I aim that arrow, I never completely connect with the other. But it's the process of trying that's significant. That's where all the messy, beautiful human stuff lies—in the space between the "you" and the "other," between the "you" and the "I."

This creative process depends entirely upon hope. I hope the next time I take aim and shoot, now that I'm more conscious of my previous misfirings, that I'll aim straighter and cleaner, and I hope more of me will find its way connecting intimately with more of you. Please don't misinterpret this sentiment as a call for some sort of commercial formula in filmmaking. On the contrary, by connecting, I'm telling a story, by telling your story revealing yourself in the telling, reading and being read back.

I learned how to read in this place. Now, not literally. That would be very bad PR, I realize that. By "reading" I mean trying to go deeper, trying to go beyond the obvious explanation, beyond the historical analysis, beyond the fact, beyond logic and certainty, beyond all those neat little unquestioned boxes the world puts in front of you like so much cold stone. The process of reading, of finding the self in the other, of searching for the human dimension, for the essence and yes, of failing miserably at that task and finding instead the searcher, the self, the questions once again.

I see this unending process of reading as a kind of Nautilus series, designed to muscularize the brain, the senses, the heart, the spirit, and these organs grow in strength and breadth throughout the years and beyond these college years until perhaps one day, when you're old and gray and stop trying so hard, they can embrace virtually every text, every experience, every "other," and maybe one day they'll analyze, synthesize, and accept entirely without judgment. At least that's what you hope in your mess of human foolishness. You hope that the subject should come to know the object so intimately that they become in fact one.

"That hope we hold is like an anchor in our lives, an anchor safe and sure." I've been carrying around that quote for ten years in memory of the Anchor Bar here in New Haven. This is where I learned to hope and to set blindly on a path here today looking already paved that leads to becoming. And when I stand here today looking at all these actual walls and these gowns and funny hats and clay pipes and all these beaming professors and libraries filled with poetry, music, and inspiration, what I read beyond the garnish is hope. That hope is like J. D. Salinger's Fat Lady.* She lives inside these Gothic monuments, she peeks out, smiles, and applauds at your discoveries—a big bright, loving, accepting smile— and it doesn't really matter whether she exists or not. It's the hope she holds for you that matters. And it's that hope that's changed me, that lives within me and makes me move toward getting better, going deeper and wanting to understand more

---

*The Fat Lady comes from J. D. Salinger's work *Franny and Zooey*.

completely. The "I" touched by the discovery of other "I"s—
that's the intangible prize, I think. The brochures kept telling
you it was the landscape that would last forever.

So it's been twelve years since I first stepped onto this
campus, and we all know what the last twelve years in America have meant. When the presidential elections rolled around
in the beginning of my freshman year, I was still too young
to vote. And by some unbelievable sick twist of fate Ronald
Reagan was elected President that November. I remember
crossing Elm Street the day after the election with this overwhelming sadness. I could barely talk; I just kept saying,
"Wait a minute, this isn't fair, I couldn't even vote." And it
felt like the end of something, and effectively it was actually
the beginning of something too. Twelve years of a national
philosphy, cruel, bad, and indifferent that shaped the following Yale generations in reaction to it. By the middle of the
eighties a distinct minority stopped being obsessed and ma-
nipulated by who was the head of the basketball team and
started paying attention to and identifying with who's left out
of the basketball team. And the dissatisfaction and frustration.
Every class that lived through the early eighties helped to
empower one silent and indifferent generation of students
who realized they were now going to have to fight for the
voice of human dignity. They knew they were going to have
to speak out for alternatives to a historically insidious disrespect for the individual's rights.

So as you'll all remember, the media seized an opportunity
to characterize these few symptoms of real consciousness as
a gigantic monster: political correctness. Soon everyone from
Time magazine to your aunt Gladys was promoting fantasies
of this bogeyman swooping into college campuses, brain-
washing their little white babies, and goose-stepping to the
music of the liberal elite. "Oh, why?" they kept saying.
"Why can't those kids just be quiet and do the hustle to the

corporate elite like we did?" And of course you were all on the inside of this debate and knew perfectly well that very little had changed. But one thing is for certain. The world you are entering into has not gotten better in the last decade. Every injustice and intolerance you can think of is becoming more and more inflamed by hard times—racism, sexism, homophobia, to name a few.

You are facing problems and crises every day that your parents couldn't even imagine—some that they could but some they couldn't imagine. Let's not forget this decade has been about living with a plague called AIDS. Your parents' generation will never know what it is to stand here today in a crowd of brothers and sisters who you have known and loved and held and laughed with like big, dumb, slobbery dogs. You stand here knowing that a lot of you are not going to make it past thirty. That's our generation. That's our reality. And if they want to call it politically correct to care about the things that touch our lives, then let them.

You have a right and a responsibility to lay claim to what touches you and affects change for the future. And that's what this incredibly privileged education is all about. You get to have a choice so that maybe in the wake of it other people can have choices too.

You get to have a voice and be an advocate for people who don't have a voice. Now does that sound patronizing and elitist? Well, it kind of is. Over the weekend you'll hear this a thousand times: You are the top 1 percent of this nation. You are the hope, the pride, the cream of the American elite, the ones who will change this country by virtue of education and a newfound adopted class and status of the mind. And if you are anything like I was, that idea will make you hysterically ill in disbelief, cynicism, and disgust. What a bunch of arrogant, elitist, patriarchal bull. You look at your friends around you, goofy from last night's revelries, passionate and undisciplined, angry and confused, and rich and poor and black and female and short and loud and eternally stoned and full of beans, and you'll say: "Yeah, who's gonna let them be on top? Who's gonna let them be sheriff of the Jell-O? All of these unfocused ideas and no clue how to direct them. Who's going to listen to us?"

Being twenty-something is all about taking it in, eating it, drinking it, and spitting out the seeds later. It's about being fearless and stupid and dangerous and unfocused and abandoned. It's about being in it, not on top of it. So I'm sure you'll laugh at these condescending clueless alumni faces like myself calling you to salute an Ivy League assumed superiority. We can't possibly be the ones to shape this nation; who the hell is going to shape us?

But the weird thing is, ten years down the road, you're thumbing through a magazine in a doctor's office; there's your buddy, helping formulate policy decisions that will make your life miserable, or tolerable. You walk down the street; there's your buddy heading an enormous *Fortune* 500 company that's just instituted spousal health care. Your kids turn on *Sesame Street*, and there's your buddy singing "The Shadow Song" with the Cookie Monster. Suddenly they're everywhere— challenging old ideas, giving their lives for peace, discovering medicine, making you laugh hysterically on a cable show, getting indicted for felonies . . . they're selling out and squeezing in; you can't escape them. Yale graduates keep affecting your world no matter how loud you turn up the MTV. They're out there wreaking havoc for eternity. And in twenty years you guys are going to be making and breaking all of our lives whether you like it or not. And I for one am happily fastening my seat belt. It's going to be a bumpy ride.

But for the time being, since you're stuck in your seats listening to me and since I have you captive and you can't move, well, I might as well take advantage of you, of your audience. To use my earlier analogy, I'm going to pull back my bow and arrow and cut out the noise and distraction and focus on sending what I believe in, what I've come to know while living in this mortally diminutive body, send my stuff, flying toward you, no apologies, no hesitations. You may discard and evade at will; as I said before, control is not my goal.

I spent my twenties just doing things. Not asking why. Just testing different muscles and never internalizing the consequences before I started. And that felt like an impossible hunger, indiscriminate and wild. I just kept putting stuff in my mouth, in my head, in my life, without ever asking myself, "Was it good for me? Was it good for my career? Was it good for the Union?"

For example, when I showed up on the set of *The Accused*,* I only read the script once. I just kept procrastinating, going out and dancing and exercising and barbecuing chicken and things like that. I knew I was desperate to play the part, but I still couldn't bring myself to really know what I was getting into. That's a good thing because if I had thought about it for five minutes, I'd have let fear and the old left brain get ahold of me. I'd have decided it just wasn't my Olympic event, that it wasn't what anyone told me I was capable of. I would've been too scared of all the things I didn't understand. And instead I forged ahead blindly because quite simply I was compelled. I had the confidence to listen to my own voice, to choose the process of becoming without really knowing what it would lead to. No stopping, no picture taking, no souvenirs.

The Accused (1988) was based on a Massachusetts rape case where five men gang-raped a woman on a pool table while being cheered on by onlookers. Foster won an Academy Award for Best Actress for her powerful performance.

The twenties for me were about learning to trust my instincts above all else. Being inside the dance without continual awareness of the choreography. That's the most essential quality you can have as an actor and a director. The ability to dive headfirst into an unknown body of water and commit to the current with a lot of faith, no hesitation, and a big, fat smile on your face.

Now somewhere along the way I started looking over my shoulder and noticing a pattern and my work starting to take a shape. It wasn't just about being hungry for more, it wasn't about being richer or having whiter teeth than the guy before. It was about completing a recognizable spiritual and psychological agenda. So yes, I recognized the method to my madness. For example, I was compelled to play characters who had been overlooked, misunderstood, marginalized, victimized, or labeled as freaks. But they survive in the end. I wanted people to recognize the humanity of these characters and decide for themselves, to redeem them, and in turn simply get better because of that self-acknowledgment and self-acceptance. Now that's perhaps very foolish and naive—so what? That's why they call it the movies.

My Yale experience has given me the luxury of choice. I've chosen to make my life, my work, my love, my characters stand for something, however small and insignificant that legacy may be. And each one of you will have your own way, your own battles, your own processes. But ultimately it's up to you alone to find the way that's appropriate for you. No one can tell you what that is because no one else has ever been there before. You find your way home again. My way has brought me toward a narrowing focus at the beginning of my thirties. I want to change the system from within the system. And that means focusing and specializing. I can't fight every monster, every ogre anymore. I've got to be precise. So you know I don't read three newspapers a day. I don't know a lot about music anymore or important current events that are shaping our nation. I don't know very much about some very basic things. But if you start talking about weird French films from the seventies or the latest studio merger, I'm liable to go off and get all sweaty and indignant and passionate. Telling stories—that's my Olympic event. That's the revolution I choose to fight in. And you're no good to the revolution if you're dead or unprepared.

So what exactly did I want to pass on to you? What personal agenda do I bring to this sort of throwing of the caps and smoking of the pipe and donning of the gown? I want you to continue living. Continue searching harder, deeper, faster, stronger, and louder and knowing that one day you'll be called upon to use all that you've amassed in the process. With that wealth of self-knowledge, you hold all of our futures in your hands. So you better make it good. You better keep your eyes open and your hearts open and find out what's beneath the surface. What moves you, what repels you, and what compels you. Become human first and identify what exactly that is later. Let how you live your life stand for something, no matter how small and incidental it may seem. Because it's not good enough to put change in the meter without questioning what the meter's doing there in the first place. It's not good enough to let life pass you by in the name of some greater glory. This is it. This is all you get. So love this life, curse this life and claim this life for your very own. Do it for yourself, do it for the Fat Lady hiding in the ivy, smiling and waving and laughing at the absurdity of all this. She'll be dancing with you tonight, jiggling her body this way and that to some funky hip-hop graduation haze. She'll go on following you year after year, sitting in the back rows, beaming proudly, loving you unconditionally, and all that she asks is that you choose the becoming. And you do that alone, but in her gaze.

Now you have fun. Breathe deeply and kick ass* in the process. Just kidding. Thank you, Yale Class of 1993, and thank you for letting me share this moment with you.

---

*Jodie Foster is the only commencement speaker in the history of Yale University to implore graduates to "kick ass" in her address.

Russell Baker

Connecticut College
May 27, 1995

Russell Baker is a two-time Pulitzer Prize–winning author,
and a nationally celebrated humorist, best known for his New
York Times *"Observer" column. A popular speaker, Baker*
always delivers an inspiring, cogent message along with a lot
of laughs. He delivered this memorable address to a rapt
audience at Connecticut College.

In a sensible world I would now congratulate the Class of
1995 and sit down without further comment. I am sure the
Class of 1995 wishes I would do so; unfortunately for the
Class of 1995, we do not live in a sensible world.

We live in a world so far more slavish in its obedience to
ancient custom than we like to admit. And ancient commencement day custom demands that somebody stand up here
and harangue the poor graduates until they beg for mercy.
The ancient rule has been: Make them suffer. I still remember
the agony of my own graduation at the Johns Hopkins University. They had imported some heat from the Sahara Desert
especially for the occasion, and the commencement orator
spoke for two and a half hours. That was in 1947.

Luckily the forces of mercy have made big gains since
then. The authorities of Connecticut College have informed
me that for me to speak longer than twenty minutes would
be regarded as cruel and inhuman punishment and that if I
go as long as thirty minutes, several strong men will mount
this platform and forcibly remove me. But if I can finish in

fifteen minutes, they will let me stay for lunch. They know their man, ladies and gentlemen; when I smell a free lunch, I go for it.

So if I do this right, you'll see the back of me before minute sixteen. This will not be easy. Condensing a graduation speech into fifteen minutes is like trying to squeeze a Wagnerian opera into a telephone booth. To do it, I had to strip away the frills. This means you don't even get any warm-up jokes. So those of you who came for the jokes might as well leave now.

All right, let's plunge ahead into the dull part. That's the part where the speaker tells the graduates to go forth into the world and then gives advice on what to do when they get out there. This is a ridiculous waste of time. The graduates never take the advice, as I have learned from long experience. The best advice I can give anybody about going into the world is this: Don't do it. I have been out there and it is a mess. I have been giving graduates this advice ever since 1967, when I spoke to a batch of them over at Bennington. That was twenty-eight years ago. Some of your parents were probably graduating there that day and went on to ignore my advice.

Thanks to the genius of my generation, I told them, it was a pretty good world out there—they went forth into it, they would mess it up. So I urged them not to go. I may as well have been shouting down a rain barrel. They didn't listen. They went forth anyhow. And look what happened. Within a year Martin Luther King and Robert Kennedy were murdered; then Nixon took us to Watergate. Draft riots. Defeat in Vietnam. John Lennon killed. Ronald Reagan and his trillion-dollar deficit.

Over the years I spoke to many graduating classes, always pleading with them: Whatever you do, do not go forth. Nobody listened. They kept right on going forth, and look what we have today: Newt Gingrich and Bill Clinton. So I will not waste my breath today pleading with you not to go forth. Instead I will limit myself to a simple plea: When you get out there in the world, try not to make it worse than it already is.

I thought it might help to give you a list of the hundred most important things you can do to avoid making the world any worse. Since I am shooting for fifteen minutes, however, you will have to make do with ten. Short as the public attention span is these days nobody could remember a hundred anyhow. Even ten may be asking too much.

You remember the old joke about how television news would have reported the Ten Commandments: "God today issued ten commandments, three of which are . . ." Here is my list, ten things to help you avoid making the world worse than it already is.

One, bend down and smell a flower.

Two, don't go around in clothes that talk. There is already too much talk in the world. We've got so many people talking there's hardly anybody left to listen. With radio and television and telephones we've got talking furniture; with bumper stickers we've got talking cars. Talking clothes just add to the uproar. If you simply cannot resist being an incompetent klutz, don't boast about it by wearing a T-shirt that says UNDERACHIEVER AND PROUD OF IT. Being dumb is not the worst thing in the world, but letting your clothes shout it out loud depresses the neighbors and embarrasses your parents.

Point three follows from point two, and it's this: Listen once in a while. It's amazing what you can hear. On a hot summer day in the country you can hear the corn growing, the crack of a roof buckling under the power of the sun. In a real old-fashioned parlor, silence so deep you can hear the dust settling on the velveteen settee. You might hear the footsteps of something sinister gaining on you. Or a heart-stoppingly beautiful phrase from Mozart you haven't heard since childhood, or the voice of somebody—now gone—whom you loved. Or sometime when you're talking up a storm so brilliant, so charming you can hardly believe how wonderful you are, pause just a moment and listen to yourself. It's good for the soul to hear yourself as others hear you. And next time, maybe, just maybe, you will not talk so much, so loudly, so brilliantly, so charmingly, so utterly shamefully foolishly.

Point four, sleep in the nude. In an age when people don't even get dressed up to go to the theater, it's silly getting dressed up to go to bed. What's more, now that you can no longer smoke, drink, or eat bacon and eggs without somebody trying to make you feel ashamed of yourself, sleeping in the nude is one deliciously sinful pleasure you can commit without being caught by the Puritan squads that patrol the nation.

Point five: Turn off the TV once or twice a month and pick up a book. It will ease your blood pressure. It might even wake up your mind. But if it puts you to sleep, you're still a winner. Better to sleep than have to watch the endless parade of body bags the local news channel marches through your parlor.

Six, don't take your gun to town. Don't even leave it home unless you lock all your bullets in a safe-deposit box in a faraway bank. The surest way to get shot, contrary to popular impression, is not to drop by the nearest convenience store for a bottle of milk at midnight, but to keep a loaded pistol in your own house. What about your constitutional right to bear arms, you say? I would simply point out that you don't have to exercise a constitutional right just because you have it. You have the constitutional right to run for President of the United States, but most people have too much sense to insist on exercising it.

Seven, learn to fear the automobile. It's not the trillion-dollar deficit that will finally destroy America; it is the automobile. Congressional studies of future highway needs are terrifying. A typical projection shows that when your generation is middle-aged, Interstate 95 between Miami and Fort Lauderdale will have to be twenty-two lanes wide to avoid total paralysis of South Florida. Imagine an entire country covered with asphalt. My grandfather's generation shot horses. Yours had better learn to shoot automobiles.

Eight, have some children. Children add texture to your life. They will save you from becoming old fogies before you're middle-aged. They will teach you humility. When old age overtakes you, as it inevitably will, I'm sorry to say, having a few children will provide you with people who will feel guilty when being accused of being ungrateful for all you've done for them. It's almost impossible nowadays to find anybody who will feel guilty about anything, including mass murder. When you reach the golden years, your best bet is children, the ingrates.

Nine, get married. I know you don't want to hear this, but getting married will give you a lot more satisfaction in the long run than your BMW. It provides a standard set of parents for your children and gives you that second income you will need when it comes time to send those children to Connecticut College. What's more, without marriage you will have practically no material at all to work with when you decide to write a book, or hire a psychiatrist.

When you get married, whatever you do, do not ask a lawyer to draw up a marriage contract spelling out how your lives will be divvied up when you get divorced. It's hard enough to make a marriage work without having a blueprint for its destruction drawn up before you go to the altar. Speaking of lawyers brings me to point nine and a half, which is: Avoid lawyers unless you have nothing to do with the rest of your life but kill time.

And finally, point ten: Smile. You're one of the luckiest people in the world. You're living in America. Enjoy it. I feel obliged to give you this banal advice because although I've lived through the Great Depression, World War II, terrible wars in Korea and Vietnam, and a half-century of Cold War, I have never seen a time when there were so many Americans so angry or so meanspirited or so sour about the country as there are today. Anger has become the national habit. You see it on the sullen faces of fashion models scowling out of magazines. It pours out of the radio. Washington television hams snarl and shout at each other on television.

Ordinary people abuse politicians and their wives with shockingly coarse insults. Rudeness has become an acceptable way of announcing you are sick and tired of it all and you're not going to take it anymore. Vile speech is justified on the same ground and is inescapable. America is angry at the press. Angry at immigrants, angry at television, angry at traffic, angry at people who are well off and angry at people who are poor. Angry at blacks and angry at whites. The old are angry at the young; the young are angry at the old. Suburbs are angry at cities; cities are angry at the suburbs. Rustic America is angry at both whenever urban and suburban invaders threaten the rustic sense of having escaped from God's angry land. A complete catalog of the varieties of bile poisoning the American soul would fill a library. The question is: Why? Why has anger become the common response to the inevitable ups and downs of national life? The question is baffling not just because the American habit even in the worst of times has been mindless optimism, but also because there is so little for Americans to be angry about nowadays. We are the planet's undisputed superpower. For the first time in six years we enjoy something very much like real peace. We are by all odds the wealthiest nation on earth, though admittedly our vast treasure is not evenly shared.

Forgive me the geezer's sin of talking about "the bad old days," but the country is still full of people who remember when thirty-five dollars a week was considered a living wage for a whole family. People whine about being overtaxed, yet in the 1950s the top income tax rate was 91 percent, universal military service was the law of the land, and racial segregation was legally enforced in large parts of the country. So what explains the fury and dyspepsia? I suppose it's the famous American ignorance of history. People who know nothing of even the most recent past are easily gulled by slick operators who prosper by exploiting the ignorant. Among these rascals are our politicians. Politicians flourish by sowing discontent. They triumph by churning discontent into anger. Press, television, and radio also have a big financial stake in keeping the country boiling mad.

Good news, as you know, does not sell papers or keep millions glued to radios and TV screens. So when you're out there in the world, ladies and gentlemen, you're going to find yourself surrounded by shouting, red-in-the-face, stomping mad politicians, radio yakmeisters, and yes, sad to say, newspaper columnists telling you, "You never had it so bad," and otherwise trying to spoil your day.

When they come at you with that line, ladies and gentlemen, give them a wink and a smile and a good view of your departing back. And as you stroll away, bend down to smell a flower.

Now it seems I have run past the fifteen-minute time limit and will have to buy my own lunch.* That's life, Class of 1995. No free lunch. My sermon is done.

---

*The speech did run longer than fifteen minutes, but lunch was still free for Mr. Baker.

Sting

Berklee College of Music
May 15, 1994

As a member of the world-renowned pop trio The Police (1978–1984) with Andy Summers and Stuart Copeland, Sting established himself as one of the world's finest, most popular musicians. Indeed his solo career has been equally successful and diverse, with influences spanning everything from jazz to country and even a Broadway musical role. Sting was awarded an honorary degree in music from the famous Berklee School of Music and spoke to graduates to share with them his musical roots and to tip them to the important roles that they as musicians would play in the world.

So I'm standing here in a strange hat and strange flowing gown in front of what looks very much like an audience, and I'm about to do something that I don't very often do, which is to make a speech in public. And I'm asking myself how I managed to end up here.

This was never any plan I'd outlined for myself. Nevertheless, I'm here, and you're all expecting something coherent and perhaps meaningful to come out of my mouth. I'll try, but there are no guarantees. And I have to say I'm a little bit nervous. You might think this strange for a man who makes his living playing in stadiums, but I often stand in the middle of a stadium full of people and ask myself the same question: "How the hell did I end up here?" The simple answer is: I'm a musician.

And for some reason I've never had any other ambition

but to be a musician. So by way of explanation, I'll start at the beginning. My earliest memory is also my earliest musical memory. I remember sitting at my mother's feet as she played the piano. She always played tango for some reason. Perhaps it was the fashion at the time; I don't know. The piano was an upright with worn brass pedals. And when my mother played one of her tangos, she seemed to be transported to another world, her feet rocking rhythmically between loud and soft pedals, her arms pumping to the odd rhythms of the tango, her eyes intent upon the sheet music in front of her.

For my mother, playing the piano was the only time I wasn't the center of her world, the only time she ignored me. So I knew something significant, some important ritual was being enacted here. I suppose I was being initiated into something, initiated into some sort of mystery. The mystery of music.

And so I began to aspire to the piano and would spend hours hammering away at atonal clusters in the delusion that if I persisted long enough, my noise would become music. I still labor under this delusion.

My mother cursed me with the fine ear of a musician but the hands of a plumber. Anyway, the piano had to be sold to help us out of a financial hole, and my career as an atonal serialist was mercifully stunted. It wasn't until an uncle of mine emigrated to Canada, leaving behind an old Spanish guitar with five rusty strings, that my enormous and clumsy fingers found a musical home, and I found what was to be my best friend. Where the piano had seemed incomprehensible, I was able to make music on the guitar almost instantaneously.

Melodies, chords, song structures fell at my fingertips. Somehow I could listen to a song on the radio and then make a passable attempt at playing it. It was a miracle. I spent hour after hour, day after day, month after month, just playing, rejoicing in the miracle, and probably driving my parents round the bend. But it was their fault in the first place. Music is an addiction, a religion, and a disease. There is no cure. There is no antidote. I was hooked.

There was only one radio station in England at the time—the BBC. And you could hear the Beatles, the Rolling Stones side by side with bits of Mozart, Beethoven, Glenn Miller, and even the blues. This was my musical education. It's eclecticism, supplemented by my parents' record collection of Rodgers and Hammerstein, Lerner and Loewe, Elvis Presley, Little Richard, and Jerry Lee Lewis. But it wasn't until the Beatles that I realized that perhaps I could make a living out of music.

The Beatles came from the same working-class background as I did. They were English, and Liverpool wasn't any fancier or more romantic than my own hometown.* And my guitar went from being the companion of my solitude to the means of my escape.

There's been a lot written about my life after that time so that I can't remember what's true and what isn't. I had no formal musical education. But I suppose I became successful by a combination of dumb luck, low cunning, and risk taking born out of curiosity. I still operate in the same way. But your curiosity in music is never entirely satisfied. You could fill libraries with what I don't know about music. There's always something more to learn.

Now musicians aren't particularly good role models in society. We really don't have a good reputation. Philanderers, alcoholics, addicts, alimony jumpers, tax evaders. And I'm not just talking about rock musicians. Classical musicians have just as bad a reputation. And jazz musicians, forget it!

But when you watch a musician play—when he enters that

*Sting's hometown is Wallsend, England.

private musical world—you often see a child at play, innocent and curious, full of wonder at what can only be adequately described as a mystery—a sacred mystery, even. Something deep, something strange. Both joyous and sad. Something impossible to explain in words. I mean, what could possibly keep us playing scales and arpeggios hour after hour, day after day, year after year? Is it some vague promise of glory, money, or fame? Or is it something deeper?

Our instruments connect us to this mystery, and a musician will maintain this sense of wonder till the day he or she dies. I had the privilege of spending some time with the great arranger Gil Evans* in the last year of his life. He was still listening, still open to new ideas, still open to the wonder of music. Still a curious child.

So we stand here today in our robes with our diplomas, our degrees of excellence. Some are merely honorary, some diligently worked for. We have mastered the laws of harmony and the rules of counterpoint, the skills of arranging and or-chestrating, of developing themes and rhythmic motifs. But do any of us really know what music is? Is it merely physics? Mathematics? The stuff of romance? Commerce? Why is it so important to us? What is its essence?

I can't even pretend to know. I've written hundreds of songs, had them published, had them on the charts. Grammys and enough written proof that I'm a bona fide successful songwriter. Still, if somebody asks me how I write songs, I have to say I really don't know. I don't really know where they come from. A melody is always a gift from somewhere else. You just have to learn to be grateful and pray that you will be blessed again some other time. It's the same with the lyrics. You can't write a song without metaphor. You can

---

*Gil Evans, 1912–1988. A popular arranger and composer, he was best known for his work with Miles Davis in the 1950s and 1960s.

mechanically construct verses, choruses, bridges, middle eights, but without a central metaphor, you ain't got nothing.

I often wonder, Where do melodies come from? Where do metaphors come from? If you could buy them in a store, I'd be the first one in the queue, believe me. I spend most of my time searching for these mysterious commodities, searching for inspiration. Paradoxically I'm coming to believe in the importance of silence in music. The power of silence after a phrase of music, for example: the dramatic silence after the first four notes of Beethoven's Fifth Symphony, or the space between the notes of a Miles Davis solo. There is something very specific about a rest in music. You take your foot off the pedal and pay attention. I'm wondering as musicians whether the most important thing we do is merely to provide a frame for silence. I'm wondering if silence itself is perhaps the mystery at the heart of music. And is silence the most perfect form of music of all?

Songwriting is the only form of meditation I know. And it is only in silence that the gifts of melody and metaphor are offered. To people in the modern world, true silence is something we rarely experience. It almost as if we conspire to avoid it. Three minutes of silence seems like a very long time. It forces us to pay attention to ideas and emotions we rarely make any time for. There are some who find this frightening.

Silence is disturbing. It is disturbing because it is the wavelength of the soul. If we leave no space in our music—and I am as guilty as anyone else in this regard—then we rob the sound we make of defining context. It is often music born from anxiety to create more anxiety. It's almost as if we're afraid of leaving space. Great music is as often about the space between the notes as it is about the notes themselves. A bar's rest is as significant as the bar of demi, semiquavers that precedes it. What I'm trying to say here is that if I am ever asked if I'm religious, I always reply, "Yes, I'm a devout musician." Music puts me in touch with something beyond intellect, something otherworldly, something sacred.

How is it that some music can move us to tears? Why is some music indescribably beautiful? I never tire of hearing Samuel Barber's "Adagio for Strings" or Fauré's "Pavane" or Otis Redding's "Dock of the Bay." These pieces speak to me in the only religious language I understand. They induce in me a state of deep meditation or wonder. They make me silent.

It's very hard to talk about music in words. Words are superfluous to the abstract power of music. We can fashion words into poetry so that they are understood the way music is understood, but they only aspire to the condition where music already exists.

Music is probably the oldest religious rite. Our ancestors used melody and rhythm to co-opt the spirit world to their purposes—to try and make sense of the universe. The first priests were probably musicians, the first prayers probably songs.

So what I am getting around to saying is that as musicians whether we're successful playing to thousands of people every night, or not so successful, playing in bars or small clubs, or not successful at all, just playing alone in the apartment to the cat, we are doing something that can heal souls, that can mend us when our spirits are broken. Whether you make a million dollars or not one cent, music and silence are priceless gifts. May you always possess them. May they always possess you.

Dan Rather

University of Texas at Austin
May 20, 1995

*Dan Rather is a television reporter, author, and five-time
Emmy Award winner. Born in Wharton, Texas, Rather
attended Sam Houston State College before joining United
Press International and the* Houston Chronicle *as a reporter.
Some of his most famous early assignments include his
coverage of the assassination of President John F. Kennedy, his
reports from Vietnam during the Vietnam War, and his
coverage of President Richard Nixon's trips to the Mideast,
China, and the Soviet Union in the 1970s. After co-anchoring*
60 Minutes *in the late 1970s, he became the anchor and
managing editor of* The CBS Evening News with Dan
Rather *in 1981.*

I am pleased and proud to be here with you all tonight. But
most especially with you graduates on your day. It is a high
honor to be asked to say a few words to you graduates at
this, one of the great moments of your lives. And to be with
those parents who are here at one of the great moments of
their lives.

I want to say a few words in the time allotted to me here:
about parents, about students, and about learning.

I remember as though it were yesterday the first time I
saw this great university, this treasure of Texas, this living,
still-growing monument to all that Texas has been and hopes
to be.

It was during the Great Depression, just before the Second

World War. It was springtime—a warm spring like this one. My father drove us—my mother, my brother and sister, and me, our whole little family—in a badly battered used car— the first car we had ever owned. We came from the Gulf Coast to see for ourselves for the first time the state Capitol and the university.

Insofar as they ever thought about it, my parents wanted their children to have a clear picture in their minds of what these places were—not just houses of power and wisdom but real buildings we could see and touch and maybe someday be a part of. No one in our family had ever been to college; precious few had ever even been in the same zip code as any college. But my parents, as I suspect is the case with yours, were determined that their children should go to college. They wanted us to see and know what they were dreaming for us, the reality that they wanted so much for us.

We didn't have a radio in that car, so we sang on the long drive from Houston. We sang songs even your parents are too young to know, the old Pappy O'Daniel ballad "Beautiful, beautiful Texas, land where the bluebonnets grow." And the old Jimmy Rodgers train song "... Texas! A state I dearly love/With the wide open spaces all about me/The moon and the stars up above." We children sang loudly because the cars that passed us on the highway might not have a radio either. But also mainly because we were proud and excited to be Texans and coming to Austin.

As we topped the last rise coming into Austin from the east, we saw for the first time the soft lights on the Capitol dome and the orange lights of the university tower. My father pulled the car over to the side of the road and stopped. And we just looked, gazed, in silence and wonder, for a long time.

The Emerald City of Oz could not have looked more beautiful to us that night. And the university was better than that, because it was *real*. Its magic castles were inhabited by men and women who quested after truth, who thought and then struggled to think better.

From that moment on the university became a symbol for me of the wisdom of Texas and a physical symbol of how *much* there was to learn.

I have savored that first glimpse of the university for a lifetime, as I shall savor this moment. I hope that you are savoring your moment tonight too. I expect you've had a busy weekend, attending parties, packing your things, saying your good-byes. But I hope you have pulled off to the side of whatever road you're on and taken a moment to look back at the tower, and the university, and your friends and teachers. These things you need to absorb deep within you.

The chances are, these are the things you'll remember longest from this weekend. What I say or do here won't matter much, nor should it. I can honestly tell you I do not remember who spoke or what about; I don't remember one word of the commencement address at my graduation from Sam Houston State Teachers College. I don't remember anything except the smiles of pride on the faces of my mother and father. Parents are always the unsung heroes at any graduation.

At some point my parents did manage to find the time to express a little healthy concern as to what I might be doing *after* graduation. I know it's possible your parents may have raised that question, calmly, once or twice, over the past few days. Just out of curiosity. No pressure. Just wondering.

Well, I do have a suggested answer. It has the added advantage of being true—for every single one of you.

You are going to be a Texan. Courtesy of this great university, you are now irrevocably connected to Texas.

I was brought up to believe—so it's way too late to try to tell me otherwise—that Texas is the greatest state. Maybe you were born here; maybe you never set foot on this hallowed soil before the day you came to this school. It doesn't matter. Being a Texan is a spiritual condition. If you weren't already, you are Texans now.

And I'm here to tell you something, my young friends: You always will be. Henceforth and forever. They can't take it away. You can't give it away. Texas will always be a part of you, and you will always be a Texan.

Being a Texan, for better and for worse, means you're going to be special for the rest of your lives. Special things are going to be expected of you. Determined, proud, tough. You remember that during World War II Winston Churchill used to flash the V for victory sign, like this. Who knows? If Churchill had flashed the hook 'em horns instead, he might've won the war in half the time.

Being a Texan means doing your best—which because you're a Texan, means naturally and modestly doing better than anyone else—and being a Texan, make no mistake, means you're doing your best all the time. Round the clock, round the year, round the rest of your life.

Being a Texan means daring. It means dreaming. It means doing. It means thinking of your community, which is your family, your town, your state, and your country.

Being a Texan is a full-time job. (I know your parents will be relieved to hear you've got a job.)

Being a Texan is serious business. Whenever this nation has been in need, it has turned to Texans. From Sam Houston to Admiral Chester Nimitz, Texans have led the way. Coming from Europe and the celebrations of the anniversary of the end of World War II, as I just recently have done, I've been reminded how many Texans served their country in that war—and served every one of us.

Starting with Dwight David Eisenhower. He was born in Texas. Never spent much time here. Just enough to count.

From Iwo Jima to Omaha Beach, Texans were among—

and often led—those who rose up to the defense of liberty. Texans came when called to champion the forces of reason and right against the forces of violence and fear, against intolerance and oppression. Hard for us to believe, how distant it has become, looking back now, how much courage, how much valor and dedication was needed to fight and win that huge two-ocean war. How much strength and sacrifice were required of the Texans in uniform and the Texans who fought the war on the home front.

The times challenged each of these men and women to dig deep, to rise early and stay late, and to do their best, which meant doing better than anyone else. The cause was just; the course was clear. Texans answered the call and met the challenge.

We may think we could never find within ourselves the character that led Texans to rise up against terrorism and dictatorship and to strike it down with justice and liberty. We may hope and pray that the time never comes that we are called upon to live up to the standards those Texans set a half century ago. I join you in that hope and prayer.

Yet I know already that the time has come. I have been traveling around Texas, around America, and around the world, and I've seen it. Every day we are all called upon to be Texans, to be the best Texans we know how to be. Already. The time to be a Texan is now.

Now, today, this minute, there are a thousand questions we as Texans must face. We cannot hide from them; to hide would be unworthy of us as Texans. It is not in the Texas character to cower. We must ask, and we must demand answers, of our leaders and of ourselves.

To take perhaps not such an obvious example: What do *you* think about the genocide in Yugoslavia and Rwanda? And what do *you* plan to *do* about it? Do you or don't you plan to inform yourself about it and, at the very least, speak out about it? Similar to what the Nazis did in World War II, reminiscent of the ghastly Holocaust, today, now, in your time, on *your* watch, science and history are again being used to "justify" the slaughter of thousands and the humiliation of many other thousands. Women are raped and tortured; children are maimed. Their only "crime," so called, is that they are of the "wrong" tribe or race or religion. These things I have seen, and these things I bear witness before you tonight.

This is a murderous outrage. I respectfully submit that it is un-American, certainly un-Texan, to duck it, dodge it, or cop out by saying, "Well, it is a long way from here, Dan Rather, and from anything I care about," or by saying, "I don't know about it, and I don't want to know."

In Rwanda, in what's left of Yugoslavia, the time to be a Texan is now.

Across Europe—in Russia, in Germany, even in France— some of the old demons of fascism, including anti-Semitism, are dancing tonight. Fascism—like communism—is totalitarian, rooted in the belief that might means right, that a *few* can rule, not by law but by violence and terrorism. In this, the comparative comfort of the post-Communist era, as we revel in the triumph of the end of the Cold War, it is easy, too easy, to overlook.

Do you know *what* fascism is? Do you know why your grandfathers and grandmothers were willing to lay down their lives to defeat it? What *do you* think about the dangerous potential for its revival? What *do* you plan to do, to say about it?

In the face of fascism the time to be a Texan is now.

And terror at home, on our own shores, in our own land, this land of the Pilgrims' pride, this land where our fathers died, by some of our own fellow Americans? With the sickening outrage of the Oklahoma City bombing murders still in the headlines and fresh in our minds and in our hearts, where do *you* stand on *these* questions: How and why were such fires of hatred lighted? And who lit them?

In the face of terror and hate and demagoguery the time to be a Texan is now.

Then there is the question of race relations in our country, this great historical experiment in multireligious, multiracial, multiethnic self-government. Are we still committed to the idea and the ideal it represents? Are you? What are *you* prepared to do to preserve it? *Can* we, with our uniquely American blend of races and cultural heritage, get along? Can we preserve our Constitution and our unity? These, my young friends, are *not* rhetorical questions. They are real. They are fundamental and go straight to the vitals of ourselves as a nation, as a people, as Americans, and as Texans.

In our beloved United States of America the time to be a Texan is now.

Those are just a few of the times that require us to be Texans, the best Texans we can be. Those are the headline-grabbing, heart-stopping, big-moment challenges facing Texas, and Texans, and our neighbors.

Other challenges may seem smaller. Your spouse is ill. Your boss is dishonest. Your neighbor is alone. Your child is crying—for you. Your child is learning—from you.

Those too are times that require a Texan. Who is to say that those challenges are less important in the long run?

I'm lucky enough to have watched a few great Texans meet such challenges.

The first is my wife, Fighting-Heart Jean Grace Goebel Rather, of Winchester, Texas. No pioneer mother ever fought more bravely for her Texan children, Robin and Danjack; no Renaissance painter ever fought more bravely for her art; no wife ever loved more bravely.

With me tonight, although you cannot see them, are two other great Texans. My parents. They were not the sort of great Texans you'd find in most history books. My father dug ditches and worked derrick floors for oil companies. My mother made dresses, waited tables, did every kind of work with her back and her hands and her heart. They did not have a lot to give us children, but we never noticed. The things they did give us were big enough. Big enough for Texas.

My parents gave us learning, and all three of their children went to college eventually. (My brother and sister kept learning, became teachers—and married teachers.)

In many ways I expect my parents weren't very different from yours. Like your parents, my parents gave us dreams. They gave us hope. They gave us love.

They were giving all those things that night years ago, when they brought us to Austin, to see what a university— *the* University *of Texas*—looked like. From the crest of a hill. In the twilight of a warm spring night.

I know my parents are watching tonight, just as they watched when I graduated from college. On a night like this. Forty-two years ago they were bursting with gratitude to my teachers. Now their gratitude is directed to you, for helping to bring this Texan full circle, back to Austin, back to the university.

Here, on the faces of your parents, I see the same proud smiles tonight.

As of now, they are the parents of Texans. (I hope that's not the only reward for their care and sacrifice!) They've done a very good job in getting you to this point. Now, when you walk out of here tonight, it's up to you to do as good a job as they've done. It's up to you to do better. That's part of what it means to come here and get an education: to learn from those who came before us.

If our parents and teachers have taught us anything, let us hope we have learned this. Every adult is a teacher to every child. Every person is a neighbor to every other person. Every American is a leader. Every Texan is a doer and a giver. Every one of us . . . is a Texan.

And the time to be a Texan . . . is now.

Thank you, good luck, and Godspeed.

Ted Turner

University of North Carolina at Chapel Hill
May 16, 1993

Ted Turner is one of the most influential and powerful businessmen and television executives in history. In 1970, Turner bought a small Atlanta television station and transformed it into WTBS, the first cable television "superstation." He later bought the Atlanta Braves baseball team and the Atlanta Hawks basketball franchise in 1976 and 1977. In 1980, Turner launched the Cable News Network (CNN), the first twenty-four-hour television news station. Among his many honors, he was named "Man of the Year" by Time *magazine in 1991 (the same year he married actress Jane Fonda). And in 1997 he committed the largest single act of charity in history by donating one billion dollars to the United Nations.*

I want to congratulate all the graduates here today and the parents and families that made tremendous sacrifices during the past four or however many years it's been, depending on the graduate students. And also to all of the faculty members and staff of the university who are responsible for all this brilliance out here in blue gowns. And I also appreciate being asked to come here today.

Your class president alluded to the fact that your education doesn't stop here today, and that's really true, particularly in the world we live in today. With technological advances coming at breakneck speed in every field today there are such tremendous changes taking place that you have to keep up and try to keep ahead of what is happening in your field. The easiest way to be a big success is to be able to anticipate what is going to happen in your field and to be there before it happens rather than after it happens because that's where the greatest fortunes and successes are made—doing something before somebody else does it.

A commencement speaker at an occasion like this is supposed to share some of the experiences that they've had and some of the thoughts that may make your lives perhaps a little easier or a little less difficult. One thing that I encourage you to do, like your basketball team, the national champion North Carolina Tar Heels, is never to quit. You can never quit. Winners never quit, and quitters never win.

Also something that I learned later in life is that I recommend and I'm campaigning for more classes on how to get along, how wives and husbands get along, and how to raise children. Not enough of that is taught in school and I recommend that after you get married, as most of you probably will, if you're having problems with your marriage, get counseling just as soon as you realize there are problems. Maybe we've got marriage counselors out here. That could've saved a marriage or two of mine earlier. Of course I wouldn't have had the chance to meet the right woman.* That's another thing. Don't lose heart. Because at fifty you might get lucky.

Every generation, at least in recent history, has had some sort of really big challenge. Going back one hundred thirty or one hundred forty years ago, it was slavery and the oncoming Civil War. And then at the turn of the century slightly after that it was women's rights and women who had been denied the vote and equality and finally got it. And that was something a lot of people worked hard on. And then

---

*Ted Turner has been married three times. The right woman to whom he refers is actress Jane Fonda, whom Turner married in 1991.

there was World War I and after that the Great Depression, which was terribly challenging as the older people in the audience will remember. Then there was World War II; then there was the civil rights movement; then there was the Cold War. But I don't think any generation has faced the challenges that your generation is going to face.

And these challenges are really, I think, twofold. From a domestic standpoint, I think that, and I want to apologize to you for this, my generation and the generation before me left you over four trillion dollars in debt, and that was a dirty rotten trick to play on you. We borrowed a lot of your money and spent it, and I personally am very sorry for it because you and your children are going to have to help pay it back. I would just recommend that you get on with it real quickly. Don't wait until it's out of control, which it is very close to being at the present time.

The other great challenge that no other generation has faced is the population explosion and the tremendous taxing that all of these people have put on our environment. In certain parts of the world the environment is collapsing. In places like Bangladesh, in Haiti, and in northern Africa, the situation has gone from bad to almost terminal. This is something that you are going to have to deal with very much in your generation.

But I think it's also very exciting, because you know there's nothing like the finals or the playoffs to really get the juices up. If the human race is going to survive past your generation, it's going to be that you made the right moves at the right times.

I intend to stay around as long as I can to report on it because I think it is the greatest story of all time. And whenever there is that kind of challenge, there's more opportunities for leadership and more opportunities to accomplish more great things than ever before. So this will be the most challenging time that any group of human beings has ever faced. And you folks with this tremendous education from this great university have got the kind of background and education that you need to tackle it.

I wish you the very best. Have a great life and great careers. Good luck to you all.

Ben and Jerry

Southampton College
May 21, 1995

Ben Cohen and Jerry Greenfield have done much more than make pints of the world's most decadent, chunky, creative new flavors of gourmet ice cream. Their Vermont-based business sets forth the prototype for business in the twenty-first century. Theirs is a business that cares about community and offers a progressive work environment that allows employees to enjoy and to share in the success of the company.

Jerry Greenfield

Graduation is a time for words of wisdom, thought-provoking words, challenging words. And that is why we have Ben with us today. I'll be speaking to you about how we reached our august positions as true ice-cream magnates.

Ben and I are old friends from junior high school. We met at Merrick Avenue Junior High School in the seventh grade, when we were the two slowest, fattest kids running around the track together. Coach Phelps was yelling at us, "Gentlemen, you have to run the mile in under seven minutes. If you don't run the mile in under seven minutes, you're gonna have to do it again!" And there were Ben and I in this little pack way behind the rest of the pack, and Ben would yell back, "Gee, Coach, if I don't run it in under seven minutes the first time, I'm certainly not going to run it in under seven the second time!" And that's when I first realized that Ben was someone I wanted to get to know.

We went through school together and graduated in 1969. It was time to go to college. Ben didn't really want to go to college. But his parents wanted him to go, so his father and his older sister filled out his applications for him and he ended up going to Colgate in upstate New York. Because they had fireplaces in the dorms and Ben thought that was really cool. Ben soon dropped out of Colgate, signed up with another school, soon dropped out of there, and then he joined up with a program called University Without Walls, a progressive, unstructured program where you don't have to go to class. The world is your campus, and you get credit for learning. And Ben dropped out of there too. Still a little too much structure.

Ben worked at various jobs: as a taxi driver in New York, a short-order cook, a night mopper, a security guard, a phone book delivery person. I, on the other hand, went to Oberlin College in Ohio, finished in four years straight, tried to get into medical school, didn't get in, got a job as a lab technician in a biochemistry research lab, reapplied to medical school, didn't get in again, and took another job as a lab technician since I already had the experience.

This is how we found each other facing the world. Gee, we thought, why don't we do something fun? We could be our own bosses, and hang out together. We thought we'd do something with food since we both liked to eat quite a bit. We picked ice cream. We didn't know anything about ice cream so we decided to continue our formal education by taking a correspondence course in ice cream. It was a five-dollar course from Penn State University that we split, so it was two-fifty apiece. They sent us a textbook in the mail. You read through the chapters of the textbook; you have tests at the end of every chapter. You're allowed to look up the answers at the end of every chapter. You mail them to your professors. They grade them and mail them back. We got a hundred percent on every test!

So we had finally found the type of education that was really suited to our learning. And we've gone on from there. Without further ado I'd like to introduce Ben with hopefully some words of wisdom.

Ben Cohen

Well, you know, for those of us who never really got a degree the way you were supposed to, the idea of picking one up without really doing any work is pretty strong. I got one before from some other college, and I checked it out and it was a degree in commercial science, and I was entitled to all the rights and privileges. I discovered afterwards there really is no degree in commercial science and it was kind of a fake honorary degree. I was quite impressed to learn that the doctorate I'm receiving today is one of Humane Letters. I'm not really sure what Humane Letters are, but I've heard of it before. So thank you for inducting me into that esteemed academic community.

I'd like to begin my remarks today with an old Indian saying: When you were born, you cried and the world rejoiced. Live your life in such a way that when you die, the world cries and you rejoice.

Well, you know the business started as Jerry said. Our idea at the beginning was to be a homemade ice-cream parlor. Then things started growing quite a bit more than we ever expected them to. When we realized we had a multimillion-dollar business here, we were a little concerned because we were becoming businessmen rather than ice-cream men. We were spending our time dealing with accountants and lawyers, hiring and firing and writing memos and stuff. And that was a lot different from making and scooping ice cream, which we had in mind. As we began to realize that what we were was businessmen, we were concerned because we saw business as a tool of economic oppression. So we said as long as we're gonna be businessmen, how can we use our business as a force for progressive social change?

We started out by looking at the definition of "business." The usual definition of "business" is an entity that produces a product or provides a service. At Ben and Jerry's we see it differently. We say that business is a combination of organized human energy plus money which equals power. I would go so far as to say that business is the most powerful force in the world. This is a new phenomenon which has occurred in my lifetime. Originally the most powerful force in the world was religion. And then the most powerful force came to be government. And today it's business. You can see this echoed in the buildings in our major cities. The oldest, most ornate building is a religious institution. The next oldest one is governmental. And today the biggest, most ornate buildings are commercial.

So business, this most powerful force in society, controls society. It controls the nature of our everyday interactions. It controls elections through campaign contributions, it controls legislation through lobbying, it controls media through ownership, and it controls the treatment of our citizens as employees and customers. And for the most part it is done within the narrow self-interest of business without a concern for the welfare of society as a whole. Except for maximizing profits, many businesses tend to be valueless. When we as employees walk into a business at nine in the morning, the message we get is to leave our values at the door. You're here to earn a living and to maximize profits, and if you have some social concerns that you want to deal with, do it at home in your own spare time and give a few dollars to whomever knocks at your door. And yet it is just when we as human beings are organized in our most powerful force as a business that we are able to deal with the social problems that confront our society, and it is just at that point that we are forbidden from doing so.

What we are discovering at Ben and Jerry's is that there is a spiritual aspect to business, just as there is to the lives of individuals. Just because the idea that the good that you do comes back to you is written in the Bible and not in some business textbook doesn't mean that it is any less valid. We are all interconnected. As we help others, we cannot help but to help ourselves.

Well, this is a pretty new consciousness for business, and it represents a real paradigm shift from a win/lose scenario, where it's business versus consumers, business versus the environment, business versus society, to a win/win scenario, where it's business working to help its consumers, business working to help society and the environment. It's a paradigm shift back to biblical values, but as a paradigm shift it meets with incredible resistance. Here's what the German philosopher Arthur Schopenauer had to say about situations like this: All truth passes through three stages. First, it is ridiculed. Second, it is violently opposed. Third, it is accepted as being self-evident.

Rosabeth Moss Cantor, writing in the *Harvard Business Review*, said that money should never be separated from its mission. It is an instrument, not an end. Detached from its values, it may indeed be the root of all evil. Linked effectively to social purpose, it can be the root of opportunity. Well, that's what we've been trying to do at Ben and Jerry's, to link it effectively to social purpose. And we've constantly been experimenting and learning, innovating, making mistakes, failing, trying again, and sometimes we succeed, sometimes we fail. But this is our effort, and this is our direction. Just as it is in coming up with new flavors. Sometimes they're great; sometimes they fail.

The object at Ben and Jerry's is to integrate a concern for society into our day-to-day business decisions. That's how we decide to come up with flavors like Rainforest Crunch that help the rain forests survive. That's how we come up with flavors like Chocolate Fudge Brownie that provides work for people in an inner-city bakery that were formerly jobless. That's how we decide to come up with flavors like Aztec Harvest Coffee where we can buy our coffee beans directly from the people who grow them from a co-op in Mexico. And that's how we decide to sell our ice cream through shops owned by nonprofit institutions located in inner-city areas in New York City, or else in Times Square.*

Martin Luther King said the stability of the large world house which is ours will involve a revolution of values to accompany the scientific and freedom revolution engulfing the earth. We must rapidly begin the shift from a thing-oriented society to a person-oriented society. When machines and computers, profit motives and property rights are considered more important than people, then the giant triplets of racism, materialism, and militarism are incapable of being conquered. A society can flounder in the face of moral and spiritual bankruptcy as it can through financial bankruptcy. So returning business to being a more caring, more spiritual entity which acts to serve society is one part of the solution to the problems that confront us today. The other is to release government from the clutches of politics, the military, and corporations.

I want to know what we have to do to get our politicians

---

*Ben and Jerry donate 7.5 percent of their pretax profits to a number of causes that benefit children, families, and disenfranchised groups.

in Washington to realize that while they are playing their picayune games, there are people out there suffering and dying through no fault of their own. Our country could be giving them a hand up, but we're not. Our politicians say they don't have the money, but there's no problem coming up with billions for the savings and loan bailout* or billions to protect oil in the Persian Gulf. It isn't fair. I refuse to hear another word about weapons systems or a space launch and keep my mouth shut. How do you look a hungry child in the face who just came home from a disintegrating, defaced, ill-equipped school through a garbage-strewn neighborhood where gunshots are an everyday occurrence, and say you don't have the money to rebuild those schools and protect those streets? It's a lie.

The threats to our society are not from without but from within. Yet we continue to spend two hundred ninety billion dollars a year on an enemy that has vanished. According to the Center for Defense Information, our country could take a hundred forty billion dollars a year out of the U.S. military budget. That would be enough money to provide for the thirty thousand children a day who are dying around the world from hunger and preventable diseases as well as provide for the one out of four children in the U.S. who are born into poverty. That would still leave one hundred fifty billion for the military, and the U.S. would still be the most powerful military force in the world. And every billion dollars that we transfer out of the military into domestic programs creates six thousand jobs to boot.

Our country, the last remaining superpower on earth, needs to learn to measure its strength not in how many people

*During the 1980s, the U.S. government backed a number of Savings and Loan institutions which failed because of bad banking practices, bad investments, and corruption of bank officials. In 1989, President Bush authorized a bailout of these institutions, which cost taxpayers hundreds of billions of dollars.

we can kill but by how many people we can feed, clothe, house, and care for. The enemy is not the poor, and the enemy is not other countries. The enemy is selfishness. The enemy is that the most powerful force in our society does not accept responsibility for the common good. The enemy is capitalism run amok. The enemy is the mentality that would have us build more jails when we already have the highest percentage of people in prison of any industrial society.

Elie Wiesel said that the opposite of love is not hate but indifference. What we are learning at Ben and Jerry's is that there is a spiritual aspect to business just as there is to the lives of individuals. As you give, you receive. As your business supports the community, the community supports your business. As you help others, you are helped in return. For people, for business, for nations . . . it is all the same.

Thank you.

George Lucas and
Steven Spielberg

University of Southern California
May 6, 1994

*Perhaps no two names loom larger in modern movie history
than George Lucas and Steven Spielberg. Lucas's* Star Wars
*trilogy ushered in the age of blockbuster movies and gave
audiences a timeless story of good versus evil that has become
permanently embedded in popular culture. Spielberg has
directed some of the most memorable and popular movies of all
time, including* Jaws, Close Encounters of the Third Kind,
Raiders of the Lost Ark *(with Lucas),* E. T., *and* Schindler's
List, *for which he received Oscars for Best Director and Best
Picture. Both graduates of USC's prestigious film school,
Lucas and Spielberg received honorary doctorates in Fine Arts
from the university in May 1994.*

George Lucas

I'd like to thank the university for this great honor. I received
my bachelor's degree here back in 1966. It seems like yesterday that I was sitting right out there. I must say, it's a lot
more exciting this time around. When my daughters heard
about this honorary degree, they took to calling me "Dr.
Daddyo." I guess that's what I'm going to be known as from
now on. Having struggled through Spanish and bonehead
English, one cannot help but ask, "How in the world did I
get here?" Well, I know how I got here: I got here with a
lot of help from my friends. When I was a cinema student,

I was lucky. Although the film department was filled with a lot of unique and rather strange individuals, we all helped each other. Of course, it was the sixties, and togetherness was the "in" thing, and competitiveness was out. But even so, there was an amazing amount of cooperation and support among the students. And this carried on after we graduated. We recommended each other for jobs, and we helped each other with our projects, and we worked on each other's scripts. We did whatever we could to help each other succeed. As a direct result of this, a great many of us did succeed. And Steven and I, over the last twenty years or so, have shared this philosophy: I truly believe that his success is my success, and my success is his success. I do not hold with the tenet, which has been popular during the last decade, "It's not enough that I succeed; my best friend must fail." With this everyone loses. With this ritual today you are officially part of the struggle. "Which struggle?" you say. In the end there is only one struggle: The struggle is to survive on the planet. The human race is struggling for survival every day, and our only weapon is knowledge. It is the shell on our backs, the poison in our fangs, and the camouflage that covers our bodies. Gaining knowledge is our only hope for survival. Passing that knowledge on to future generations is our most important challenge. Our society needs a good educational system. You have graduated, so you may now start to learn. You must learn so that you will teach. We have a long way to go before we are living in a symbiotic relationship with this planet. Symbiosis is two dissimilar organisms living together—especially when the association is mutually beneficial. It is the most important thing that I learned from my friend here at the film school. It is the most important thing we must learn if we are to survive as a society. Thank you very much.

Steven Spielberg

I guess this means that after twenty-five years I'm finally getting out of college. I'd like to thank my colleague and friend George Lucas and the University of Southern California, both of whom made it possible for me to be here today. George said to me when we made *Raiders of the Lost Ark*, "If this film makes any money, I want you to start putting money back into USC." He said, "You know the film industry takes so much from USC, but we never as a film industry seem to put anything back into our universities." And I think he's absolutely right: If we drink from the well, we have to replenish the well. I think it's appropriate to talk about values at this time and place. We're living in a time some might describe as valueless. Genocide is taking place in Bosnia and, recently, in Rwanda. People are continuing to starve in Somalia, while warlords stop the flow of relief aid. There are neo-Nazis in Europe, and random acts of violence plague every one of our cities in America. And here we are, in a city named for the angels, at a place in which curiosity is encouraged and also valued. Are we naive in wanting to believe in things we cannot see and in trying to find them? My films have often been accused of—or, as I like to think, applauded for—having childlike qualities. I do believe that the greatest quality that we can possess is curiosity, a genuine interest in this world around us. The most used word—and I have five kids, so I know what I'm talking about—the most used word in a child's vocabulary is "why?" A child doesn't blindly accept things as they are, doesn't blindly believe in limits, doesn't blindly believe in the words spoken by some authority figure like me. "Don't do that!" They say, "Why?" "Act like everyone else!" "Why?" From this simple question and such basic curiosity, great acts are born. A child is told to do what he's told, and from that "why?" is born a lone young man facing down a government tank in Tiananmen Square. A child is told to hate people who are different from him, and from him and his "why?" democracy is born in South Africa. A child is told that violence is the answer, and from his "why?" four angels swoop down and lead a half-dead truck driver to safety right here in this city that is indeed full of angels—as invisible as they sometimes are. With curiosity comes fearlessness. A child will walk up to a hot stove and touch it. Does it hurt? Yes! Was it a stupid thing to do? Well, kind of. But you have to admire the daring of that child. His brave spirit is the angel inside each of us, the force that often seems to shrink as we grow bigger. Still, it's there, and we have a responsibility to keep it strong, just as we work our bodies to keep the muscles from atrophying. It doesn't matter what path we take; we have to remain curious and fearless. We have to look at the world and question what we see. We have to be unafraid to say no and change what is unacceptable. Each of us has a responsibility to do it. Basic human values, I think, are as simple as a child's tale. It's "once upon a time," but I believe that the time is now, and is "happily ever after" as well. I don't think I'm being naive. After all, I live in the City of Angels. And you who are about to become the custodians of the future of my children, please treat my kids, and all the kids, as if they were your own. Thank you.

Carl Sagan

Wheaton College
May 20, 1993

*Carl Edward Sagan was one of America's most well-known
and respected astronomers. After receiving his doctorate in
astrophysics from the University of Chicago, Sagan taught at
Harvard University and served as an astrophysicist at the
Smithsonian Astrophysical Laboratory before becoming the
director of the Laboratory for Planetary Studies at Cornell
University in 1969. In 1980, he produced and hosted the
popular television series* Cosmos, *a series that established him
as one of the most widely recognized scientists in the world.
Sagan specialized in studying the possibilities of extraterrestrial
life and also became a strong proponent of nuclear disarmament
and an expert on the global effects of thermonuclear war. He
died of cancer in 1994.*

Humans have always had rites of passage for critical, transitional moments in our life histories. This is a tradition going back not just hundreds of thousands of years but millions.

Our genus, the genus *Homo,* is a few million years old. Our species, *Homo sapiens,* is a few hundred thousand years old. We arose in the savannas of East Africa. We were hunters and gatherers. No fixed abode, no property, we followed the game. Our numbers were few. Our powers were feeble. But we had technology.

We humans have been technologists from the beginning. It's true that the early technology was stone tools—and fire (a technology, incidentally, that we still haven't entirely mastered). If you look in the paleoanthropological record in East Africa, you can find that different places have different stone-hewing traditions. We can tell from how the axes and other tools have been flaked and hewn that they taught (these skills) one way in one spot and a thousand kilometers away quite a different way.

So that immediately means there had to be schools. And there had to be instruction. There had to be tests. There probably were failing grades. There probably was a disgusted throwing away of the inept tools. And there probably were graduation ceremonies, in which the elders stood around and congratulated those of both sexes who had succeeded in mastering the technology and the knowledge necessary for the future.

Today there are nearly five and a half billion of us. We are all over the planet, even on the ocean floor and a couple of hundred miles up in space now and again. Our technology has developed into formidable, maybe even awesome powers. This technology is both our opportunity and our danger. It's a double-edged sword—just as fire was from the beginning. . . .

We owe our lives—not just the quality of our lives, but the existence of our lives—to technology. Most people on earth would be dead if not for modern agriculture and modern medicine. At the same time, that technology permits weapons of mass destruction, permits inadvertent changes in the environment that sustains us all.

Clearly before us is the very dicey job of using these enormous powers wisely. This is something that we haven't had much experience in because we've never had powers this great. The capability both for good and for evil is unexcelled. And that means that this generation—you young women and men—has an absolute key role to play in the long adventure of the human species.

Because of the newness of coeducation . . . I want to share a few thoughts with you. . . . We are very close relatives of the chimpanzees. We share 99.6 percent of active genes with chimpanzees, which means there's a lot about us we can learn from chimps. Now it's clear that chimp society is—how shall I say?—testosterone ridden. By no means all, but a great deal of the aggression and intimidation is something the males feel especially comfortable and happy with.

In times of stress and crowding there's something very interesting that happens. This is brought out, for example, in the Arnhem colony of chimps in the Netherlands. The males, when they get annoyed, use rocks and stones. They like to throw things. The females are not into missiles. In times of crisis the males can be seen gathering lots of stones—their arms full, their fists clenched—to carry over and throw at their adversaries. The females walk over to these stone-laden males and pry their fingers open, take the stones out, and deposit them on the ground. Sometimes the males get huffy and regather the stones, whereupon the females do it again— sometimes three, four times—until [the males] get the point.

I have a feeling that the hereditary predisposition for females as mediators and peacemakers is in the 99.6 percent of the genes we share with the chimps. And that leads me to wonder what the world would be like if women played a role proportionate to their numbers. I don't mean just the occasional woman prime minister who beats the boys at their own game. I mean real, proportionate sharing of power. I mean half, not a few percent, of the members of the Senate— women. I mean half, not zero, of the succession of Presidents being women. I mean half the Joint Chiefs of Staff as women. I mean half of the chief executive officers of major corporations as women.

Maybe it would change nothing. Maybe under these circumstances, the institutions predetermine human behavior, and it doesn't matter whether you're male or female; if you're chairman of the Joint Chiefs of Staff, you have an attitude, and it doesn't matter what brought you to it. But I like to think that's not the case, that in a world in which women truly share power . . . we would have a more just, more humane, and more hopeful future. Maybe this is just a pipe dream. But it's a kind of fantasy I couldn't help but have in thinking about this class.

You've been given, in your four years here, some of the tools to preserve and, where necessary, to change the society and the global civilization. No one says this is easy. There are enormous forces of inertia and resistance to any change at all. And there are those who benefit and prosper from there being no change. Nevertheless, it's clear that our civilization is in trouble, that the current way we do things is not going to get us out of trouble, that significant changes are necessary. And I hope you will make them.

One of the most important tools is skeptical or critical thinking. Put another way, equip yourself with a baloney detection kit. Because there is an enormous amount of baloney that has to be winnowed out before the few shining gems of truth can be glimpsed. And a lot of that baloney is proffered by those in power. That's their job. Part of the job of education is to be able to tell what's baloney and what's not.

The urgency you feel to make changes is just the extent that change will be made. Don't sit this one out. Don't play it safe. Understand the world, and change it where it needs to be changed. Where it doesn't, leave it alone. Make our society better. Make a world worthy of the children that your generation will bear.

II

Be a Human Being First

*Let the fact that you are black or yellow or
white be a source of pride and inspiration to
you. Draw strength from it.*

—COLIN POWELL

John Grisham

Mississippi State University
May 16, 1992

*A former attorney and Mississippi state politician, John
Grisham rocketed to bestsellerdom in 1991 with his novel* The
Firm, *which spent forty-seven weeks on the* New York Times
*bestseller list and has been translated into no fewer than twenty-
nine languages. Despite his overwhelming success, Grisham has
always remained true to the values that shaped his life and
work. In this speech at his alma mater, Mississippi State
University, a humble Grisham reminds graduates to remain
open to life's unexpected opportunities.*

Thank you, Dr. Zacharias, for those kind words, and thank
you especially for this privilege to be here at this moment to
address the 1992 graduates of Mississippi State. It is an honor
for me to be here on this campus of this university that I
love so dearly.

To the graduates, congratulations on this day. Your hard
work and perseverance have brought you to this point, and
you are to be commended. Congratulations are also in order
for your parents and families and friends, and make sure you
give them all a big hug before today is over. Tell your parents
thanks and you love them. Take plenty of pictures. It's a
great day, and one you can never repeat.

Commencement speeches are usually given by people who
are either old or wise. I am neither. I'm here because I've
written three books, and because these books have been purchased and read and enjoyed by many people. And I'm very

grateful for this. And if you've bought the books, I say thank you. My children say thank you.

Commencement speeches usually fall into three categories. First, you have Peace Corps speeches in which the speaker attempts to motivate you, the graduates, to forsake jobs and money and credit cards and ignore your student loans, and go off to the Third World and teach starving people how to grow food. There's nothing wrong with the Peace Corps. I wish I had joined. There's nothing wrong with the Peace Corps speech, except few people listen. Second, you have the good citizen speech in which the speaker attempts to motivate you to become productive, vote properly, run for office, enjoy paying taxes and in general build a new society. The world is at your feet. The future is yours. You can move mountains, etc., etc. Though I really can't remember, I think I heard one of these fifteen years ago when I sat where you are now. It was quite dull. Third, you have the current affairs speech in which a distinguished politician or statesman or diplomat talks about the current mess in world politics and what we should do to solve the problems. I served seven years in the state legislature, so I cannot be classified as a distinguished politician. And if you watch CNN, then you know as much about the world as I do.

So, I will ignore tradition and try to say something you might remember for more than twenty-four hours.

When I sat out there fifteen years ago, I was rather smug and confident, perhaps even a bit arrogant because I, at the age of twenty-two, had already figured out my life. I had it all planned, and was certain things would fall neatly into place. I had earned my degree in accounting. I had been accepted to law school where I planned to study tax law and one day soon make lots of money representing rich people who didn't want to pay taxes. My goal was to become a successful lawyer, and there was no doubt it would happen. Everything was planned.

For those of you who have read *The Firm*, you might be shocked to learn that I was not heavily recruited when I finished law school. There were no law firms throwing money at me. In fact, no one offered me a job.

Undaunted by this, I returned to my hometown of South-haven, hung out my shingle and declared myself ready to sue. I worked hard, treated people fairly, and soon was very busy.

In those days, I never thought about writing books. I had never taken a course in creative writing, never studied the craft, never thought about being an author. I was a lawyer, and then I became a lawyer and a legislator. There were political aspirations, and I dreamed of building a big law firm. Life was pretty much on track, and it was good.

But one day, quite by accident, I stumbled into a court-room in Hernando, Mississippi, and witnessed something that would eventually change my life. I didn't realize it at the time, and that's usually the way it happens.

What I witnessed inspired me to create in my imagination a courtroom drama set in a small town in Mississippi. It could be Starkville or Oxford, Ripley or West Point, Kosciusko or Brookhaven. You know the town because you've lived there. In 1984, I wrote the first page of the first chapter of *A Time to Kill*. It was a hobby, nothing more. Three years later, I sent the completed manuscript to New York, and immediately wrote the first page of the first chapter of a story that would eventually become *The Firm*. It was just a hobby.

But that was about to change. Good luck was about to strike. Opportunity was determined to interfere. *The Firm* caught the attention of some publishers and some movie pro-ducers, and a year after the manuscript arrived in New York,

I abruptly quit law and said good-bye to politics. I was suddenly bored with these vocations. My wife and I sold our house in the suburbs and moved to a farm outside Oxford.

Fifteen years ago I had it all planned, and thank goodness it didn't work.

If you're sitting out there now with a nice, neat little outline for the next ten years, you'd better be careful. Life may have other plans. Life will present you with unexpected opportunities, and it will be up to you to take a chance, to be bold, to have faith and go for it. Life will also present you with bad luck and hardship, and maybe even tragedy, so get ready for it. It happens to everyone.

In a few hours, you will say good-bye to each other and scatter. Many of you will not return here for a long time. Four years passed before I came back, but as time has gone by, I find myself drawn back to this place more and more. If you love MSU now, you will love it more ten years from now. And you'll find yourself returning for almost any reason, and walking across the campus wondering where the years have gone. I come back now as often as I can to give talks, read from the books, and yes, to watch baseball. Not far from here is a dilapidated pickup truck that a friend purchased for a hundred dollas and spray painted by hand. It has no engine, and the tires are flat. Someone installed a few rows of benches, and I am happiest when I'm sitting on top of it watching the Bulldogs play. Time, deadlines, telephones, and appointments are all very unimportant in the left field lounge, and that's one reason I keep coming back. There are other reasons.

Barbara Bush

Wellesley College

June 1, 1990

Barbara Bush spent twelve years in presidential politics as the wife of George Bush. This speech, delivered at Wellesley College, caused quite a controversy at the time. More than 150 Wellesley students signed a petition objecting to Mrs. Bush's participation, claiming that as a Smith College dropout, and as a homemaker, she was not a suitable role model for today's career woman. In addition, Barbara Bush was joined on the podium by Raisa Gorbachev. The stylish and respected Russian First Lady was visiting the United States with her husband, Mikhail Gorbachev, the architect of glasnost.

I am really thrilled to be here today, and very excited, as I know you must be, that Mrs. Gorbachev could join us.

These are exciting times. They are exciting in Washington, and I have really looked forward to coming to Wellesley. I thought it was going to be fun; I never dreamed it was going to be this much fun. More than ten years ago, when I was invited here to talk about our experiences in the People's Republic of China, I was struck by both the natural beauty of your campus . . . and the spirit of this place.

Wellesley, you see, is not just a place . . . but an idea . . . an experiment in excellence in which diversity is not just tolerated but is embraced.

The essence of this spirit was captured in a moving speech about tolerance given last year by a student body president of one of your sister colleges. She related the story by Robert

Fulghum about a young pastor who, finding himself in charge
of some very energetic children, hits upon a game called Gi-
ants, Wizards, and Dwarfs. "You have to decide now," the
pastor instructed the children, "which you are . . . a giant, a
wizard, or a dwarf."

At that a small girl tugging at his pants leg asked, "But
where do the mermaids stand?"

The pastor tells her there are no mermaids. "Oh, yes, there
are," she said. "I am a mermaid."

Now this little girl knew what she was, and she was not
about to give up on either her identity or the game. She
intended to take her place wherever mermaids fit into the
scheme of things. Where do mermaids stand? All of those
who are different, those who do not fit into boxes and
pigeonholes. "Answer that question," Fulghum wrote, "and
you can build a school, a nation, or a whole world."

As that very wise young woman said, diversity, like anything worth having, requires effort. Effort to learn and respect
difference, to be compassionate with one another, to cherish
our own identity . . . and to accept unconditionally the same
in others.

You should all be very proud that this is the Wellesley
spirit. Now I know your first choice for today was Alice
Walker, known for *The Color Purple*. Instead you got me,
known for the color of my hair! Alice Walker's book has a
special resonance here. At Wellesley each class is known by
a special color . . . and for four years the Class of '90 has
worn the color purple. Today you meet on Severance Green
to say good-bye to all of that and to begin a new and very
personal journey. A search for your own true colors.

In the world that awaits you beyond the shores of Lake
Waban,* no one can say what your true colors will be. But

---

*Wellesley College is located on Lake Waban.

this I do know. You have a first-class education from a first-class school. And so you need not, probably cannot, live a paint-by-numbers life. Decisions are not irrevocable. Choices do come back. And as you set off from Wellesley, I hope that many of you will consider making three very specific choices.

The first is to believe in something larger than yourself. Get involved in some of the big ideas of our time. I chose literacy because I honestly believe that if more people could read, write, and comprehend, we would be that much closer to solving so many of the problems that plague our nation and our society.

Early on I made another choice, which I hope you will make as well. Whether you are talking about education, career or service, you are talking about life. And life must really have joy. It's supposed to be fun.

One of the reasons I made the most important decision of my life . . . to marry George Bush . . . is because he made me laugh. It's true, sometimes we've laughed through our tears. But that shared laughter has been one of our strongest bonds. Find the joy in life, because as Ferris Bueller said on his day off, "Life moves pretty fast, ya don't stop to look around once in awhile, ya gonna miss it!" I am not going to tell George you clapped more for Ferris than you did for George!

The third choice that must not be missed is to cherish your human connections, your relationships with family and friends. For several years, you've had impressed upon you the importance of your career of dedication and hard work, and of course that's true. But as important as your obligations as a doctor, lawyer, or business leader will be, you are a human being first, and those human connections with spouses, with children, with friends are the most important investments you will ever make.

At the end of your life you will never regret not having

passed one more test, not winning one more verdict, or not closing one more deal. You will regret time not spent with a husband, a child, a friend, or a parent.

We are in a transitional period right now, a fascinating and exhilarating time, learning to adjust to the changes and the choices we men and women are facing. As an example I remember what a friend said on hearing her husband complain to his buddies that he had to baby-sit. Quickly setting him straight, my friend told her husband that when it's your own kids, it's not called baby-sitting!

Maybe we should adjust faster; maybe we should adjust slower. But whatever the era, whatever the times, one thing will never change: Fathers and mothers, if you have children, they must come first. You must read to your children. Your success as a family, our success as a society depends not on what happens in the White House but on what happens inside your house.

For over fifty years it was said that the winner of Wellesley's annual hoop race would be the first to get married. Now they say the winner will be the first to become a CEO. Both of those stereotypes show too little tolerance for those who want to know where the mermaids stand. So I want to offer you today a new legend. The winner of the hoop race will be the first to realize her dream . . . not society's dream . . . her own personal dream. And who knows? Somewhere in this audience may even be someone who will one day follow in my footsteps and preside over the White House as the President's spouse. I wish him well!

Well, the controversy ends here. But our conversation is only beginning. And a worthwhile conversation it has been. So as you leave Wellesley today, take with you deep thanks for the courtesy and honor you have shared with Mrs. Gorbachev and with me. Thank you. God bless you, and may your future be worthy of your dreams.

Colin Powell

Fisk University
May 4, 1992

A career military officer who obtained the rank of four-star general, in 1989 Colin Powell became the first African-American to serve as chairman of the Joint Chiefs of Staff. After his retirement from the U.S. Army in 1993 he was widely discussed as a presidential candidate in 1996 but ultimately decided not to run for office. Speaking at Fisk University in the wake of the Los Angeles riots, Powell discusses overcoming racism in America. Among the many in attendance at this memorable speech was Powell's wife, Alma, a Fisk alumna.

Mr. President, trustees of Fisk University, distinguished guests, platform guests, alumni, faculty, parents, family and, yes, graduates of the Class of 1992—it is a great day for you, isn't it!

Now, as you heard my biography being read, you know why I'm here today: I'm Alma Vivian's husband.

I graduated after she did. I graduated from City College of New York in 1958. Before you start wondering about this, I'm older, she's smarter.

The first issue I want to deal with this morning has to do with what's in the minds of the graduating seniors, the question that's in the mind of graduating seniors around the country at commencement time. And that is: How long is this guy going to talk?

How long are we stuck here before we can get this on and be graduated and be on our way?

They want it short. Get it done. Let's go.

The parents, however, have a different view. That's right. They traveled a long way. They waited for four years. They want their money's worth! As far as they are concerned, I ought to be here an hour or two!

Faculty members have a different idea. One of the faculty members surely was responsible for thinking up the idea of asking General Powell to come here. And he wants me to speak long enough so it looks like a sensible decision but not so long that he has to leave town before the next faculty meeting.

Meanwhile, I'm stuck with the paradox of how long to speak. And it's going to be a function of how well you receive my remarks, students. So, if you are nice and receptive and if I hear a lot of applause, we'll be out of here quickly.

Coming here on the airplane, my staff showed me a little clipping out of the weekend newspaper. There was a picture of me next to this clipping.

The little article—it was in *USA Today* magazine—and it said, "General Powell, we know you're speaking at Fisk University. Don't worry about what you say because no one is going to remember what you say anyway."

I couldn't believe this.

So I asked Alma, "What did your commencement speaker say thirty-five years ago?"

And she said, "Say what?"

I said, "Who was your commencement speaker thirty-five years ago?"

And she didn't have a clue.

Now you are not going to embarrass me thirty-five years from now when I come back. So my name again is GENERAL POWELL—P.O.W.E.L.L.

Alma may not have remembered who her commencement speaker was, but she certainly remembered other things about Fisk:

She told me how, as a sixteen-year-old when she arrived here, she had never seen Fisk, so of course she was worried when she arrived on campus. But her worry and her concern disappeared at once because she fell in love with Fisk the moment she saw it. And the marvelous teachers and the superb education that they delivered increased her affection over the years.

And she told me about the way it was thirty-five years ago, about the dresses and the high heels the ladies wore to class, and about the handbook for the ladies which Fisk issued and which laid down the dress code.

She told me about the Oval and how it was the center of campus life, and about Jubilee Hall and about the Jubilee Singers touring all over the world.

She told me about the soldiers from Fort Campbell and the medical students from Meharry—she said she had never seen so many good-looking men in one place at one time.

And finally in her recollection of her college days, Alma Vivian let me know that she was utterly charmed by Fisk and that the passage of thirty-five years had not dimmed the warm glow of love she feels for this wonderful place. I know your memories thirty-five years from now will be the same.

To the faculty and administration of Fisk University, my congratulations to you for having done it again, for having performed this magic one more time. The results of your work and the evidence of the talent and dedication that you brought to that work are sitting here before us. You must feel a great sense of pride along with the pride that the graduates and their families feel.

To the families—mothers, fathers, wives, husbands, children, sisters, brothers, grandparents, aunts and uncles, all assembled here today—I know what is in your hearts: love, pride . . . and RELIEF!

Alma and I have attended two commencements of our own, and this coming Sunday we will go to our final commencement—for our daughter, Annemarie.

I'm proud to say—and very happy to say—that earlier this year I wrote the last check to a college after ten years of writing checks. Amen!

And of course, to the graduates, my heartiest congratulations. Your accomplishments are soon to be rewarded. Your hard work, commitment, and perseverance have paid off. You can take enormous pride in your achievement. I know this will be a red-letter day in your memories, a very, very special day for the rest of your lives.

This is a very special day for me also.

It's special because I get to look out over some of the most talented young people in America getting ready to march off and tackle the toughest problems this world can throw at them.

I have to marvel as I think back over the last thirty-five years at what an incredible world you are entering compared to the world Alma and I faced.

We graduated as the Cold War was heating up. Its lethal arsenals of nuclear weapons were growing ever more ominous. The world at that time seemed full of gloom and despair.

You graduate as that Cold War has ended and as finally we step back from nuclear Armageddon and cut those nuclear arsenals. You enter a bright, hopeful world full of promise and excitement.

We graduated as the shadow of communism darkened whole sections of the globe.

You graduate as communism lies dying. Its few remaining disciples are international basket cases.

We graduated as the chains enslaving Eastern and Central Europe were drawing ever tighter. They had even built a terrible wall in Germany.

You graduate as the power of the people has swept away the chains, torn down the wall, unified Germany, and put the dictators in Moscow out of business.

You graduate as democracy and the rule of law are sweeping more and more of the world into their embrace.

We graduated as Nelson Mandela stood trial for treason in South Africa. In 1964 he would be put to jail for what they thought was life.

You graduate with Nelson Mandela as a free man! And he and President de Klerk and other enlightened leaders are working together to destroy apartheid once and for all.

I graduated to join an Army that was very large and getting ready to grow even larger. It was a Cold War Army.

You graduate as we are taking America's Army and armed forces to the lowest level in fifty years. This will be a post–Cold War force. We will spend less money on defense. We are going to pay a peace dividend to benefit other parts of our society.

Yes, the contrasts between the world you enter today and the world Alma and I entered many years ago are stark indeed.

But perhaps nowhere is the contrast more stark than in the lives of African Americans then and now.

Alma and I graduated as the civil rights movement was beginning to gather steam under the forceful leadership of Dr. Martin Luther King, Jr., and others. African Americans, living separate and *un*equal lives, were setting out to change the American scene.

You graduate as their efforts have resulted in a thousand successes—in legal rights, in housing rights, in education, in government, and yes, in my beloved armed forces.

The young black captain just back from Vietnam thirty years ago, who couldn't get a hamburger at a Georgia restaurant unless he went to the back window, has become chairman of the Joint Chiefs of Staff of America's armed forces.

Alma and I, and so many others here, lived through this struggle in which African Americans finally began to win their full legal rights as citizens of America. We watched it happen. We were young adults like you when all of this change began.

And how did this change in the lives of black Americans, African Americans, come about?

It came about through the sweat and tears and sacrifice of thousands of African Americans. It came about on the strong backs of black men and women who struggled mightily for our future.

As a member of America's armed forces I climbed on those strong backs. I climbed on the backs of the Tuskegee Airmen, the Buffalo Soldiers, and other black military units, and on the backs of strong men, famous men like Benjamin O. Davis, Jr., and Chappie James, Jr.

Alma climbed on the strong backs she found right here on this inspired campus. And your president climbed on the strong backs he found in the fields of education, economics, and business and corporate management.

We all climbed hard. And all of us have to remember the brave people who went before and upon whose backs we climbed. All of us have to remember where we came from and what it was like then if we are to understand where we are heading and how to get there.

We also must remember that it could only have happened in America. America is the only country in the world that thrives incessantly to make the dream of America the reality of America.

Last week's scenes from Los Angeles and a dozen other

cities tell us vividly that we still have a long way to go before that dream becomes reality.

As I saw those pictures on my television set, my heart hurt. I know that your hearts hurt. I didn't want to believe what I was seeing.

Violence—by the police or by the mob—is not the answer. Our hearts hurt because of that violence. And our hearts hurt because as we watched the tragic events in Los Angeles unfold, we were thinking: No, not again. We can't let this happen again. It shouldn't be, we've come too far for this.

But it did happen. And we see once again what a long way we still have to go.

Because the problem goes beyond Rodney King. The problem goes beyond Los Angeles. It goes beyond the trial of those four officers.

The problem goes to the despair that still exists in the black community over the inability of black Americans to share fully in the American dream.

Too many African Americans are still trapped in a cycle where poverty, violence, drugs, bad housing, inadequate education, lack of jobs, and loss of faith combine to create a sad human condition. A human condition that cannot be allowed to continue if this nation is to hold its rightful place in the world.

We have an American problem. It can only be solved by all Americans working together.

As Rodney King himself said so powerfully the other day, "Please, we can get along here. . . . We've just got to. . . . We're all stuck here for a while. . . . Let's try to work it out. . . . Let's try to beat it. . . ."

Ladies and gentlemen, I say to you we must beat it. We must work it out. We must *believe* we can work it out. If I didn't believe to the depths of my heart that we could work it out, I wouldn't be able to call myself an American.

We've gotten through tough times like this before.

In 1963 John F. Kennedy was assassinated. In April 1968 Martin Luther King was gunned down in Memphis, and our cities were in flames. Two months later Bobby Kennedy was murdered.

The reason we were able then to overcome such tragedies is that we have a political system that can respond, that accommodates change, that is always moving forward.

The resilience of our system, our ability to change, our respect for human rights and respect for the rule of law help us to weather any storm, to overcome any difficulty. We can bounce back.

What we must never lose is faith. Faith that in the end right will prevail. Faith in the basic goodness of America and in the basic goodness of Americans.

We must remember that America is a family. There may be differences and disputes in our family but we must not allow the family to be broken into warring factions.

In a few moments you will become members of that family. Here's what I want you to do.

First, I want you to believe in yourself. You have to know that you are capable, that you are competent, that you are good. Your family and Fisk University have seen to that. But *you* have to believe it. I want you to believe that there is nothing—NOTHING—you cannot accomplish by hard work and commitment. Let nothing or no one ever destroy that belief you have in yourself.

Second, I want you to believe in America with all your heart, with all your mind, with all your soul, and with all your body. I've traveled around this world, and I've seen a hundred countries, and I've got to tell you there is no better place or system on earth than that which we enjoy here in America.

America is the hope and promise of the world. We are still, as Abraham Lincoln said, "the last, best hope of earth."

Third, I want you to find strength in your diversity. Let the fact that you are black or yellow or white be a source of pride and inspiration to you. Draw strength from it. Let it be someone else's problem, but never yours. Never hide behind it or use it as an excuse for not doing your best.

We all have to live here together—Asian Americans, African Americans, Hispanic Americans, all of us.

Divided, fighting amongst ourselves, walking separate lines of diversity, we are as weak as newborn babies.

Together, intertwining our many differences and diversities into a mosaic of strength, we will prevail over the darkness of racism. I want you to love one another, I want you to respect one another, see the best in each other. Share each other's pain and joy.

I want you to fight racism. I want you to rail against it. We have to make sure that it bleeds to death in this country once and for all.

As you move forward, I want you to remember those who are still struggling. We must reach back, we must all reach down, we must all work together to pull our people, to pull all Americans out of the violence, out of the dank and soul-damning world of drugs, out of the turmoil of our inner cities. As we climbed on the backs of others, so must we allow our backs to be used for others to go even higher than we have.

Finally, I want you to raise strong families. I want you to create families and raise children who are God-fearing, who are loving, who are clean, and who are determined to do even better than their parents.

As you raise your families, remember the worst kind of poverty is not economic poverty; it is the poverty of *values*. It is the poverty of *caring*. It is the poverty of *love*.

The other evening Alma and I were privileged to be with Maya Angelou. She talked about her upbringing in Stamp, Arkansas. She told us something her grandmother had said to her many years ago. Her grandmother had said, "Girl, when you cross this threshold, you're going to be *raised*."

So raise your children. Treasure them. Love them. They are our future. We cannot let the generation in front of us go to waste.

To look out at you gives me enormous hope. You look so competent, so strong, so young, so committed, so ready to take on the future, difficult times and all.

Looking at you gives me the same feeling of pride that I get when I look at our soldiers, our sailors, our airmen and marines and coast guardsmen. I know when I see them that there is nothing they can't handle, no difficulty they can't overcome, no challenge they don't relish, no mission they can't perform.

Very soon you too will be soldiers. Soldiers in the exciting struggle of life. Soldiers for education. Soldiers for business. Soldiers for science. And, above all, soldiers for a better America.

I believe in this great land that God blessed and called America—because it is full of young men and women like you. Men and women who will keep this nation moving on down the road to glory, its beacon of freedom lighting up all the dark places of the world until there is no darkness left.

We're counting on you! We're counting on you!

Thank you so very much for letting me share this special day of your lives.

Congratulations, good luck, God bless you, and remember Fisk!

Robert Redford

Claremont Graduate University
May 13, 1995

*Robert Redford is one of America's most popular and
recognized actors. He received an Academy Award for Best
Director for his directorial debut,* Ordinary People *(1980),
and directed the highly acclaimed* A River Runs Through It
(1992) and Quiz Show *(1994). A longtime political activist,
especially on issues regarding the environment, Redford stresses
the importance of taking part in the political process in this
commencement address.*

Thank you. I am honored to be here. I'm here because I have
a great regard for this school, and also this is where I grew
up—in the Los Angeles area. For better or for worse, it's
what I would call the place I grew up.

What I'm not going to do is—because it feels too awkward
and I don't really know how effective it is—I'm not going
to stand here and preach or pontificate about answers to
solutions or whatnot. The last time that I spoke on a campus
was at Rutgers University. The reason I spoke was that
Dukakis was running against Bush, and Bush had recently
gone out and advertised that he was the "environmental President." That was pretty tough for me to swallow, so I went
out and supported Dukakis to draw attention to the environment. So I spoke at Rutgers University.

There were about seven thousand students there. I got
pretty worked up about the issue, and I spoke from the heart
with very carefully prepared thoughts. The media was there,

and it was a pretty well-covered event because it was kicking off Dukakis's last swing around the country. When I was done and had sort of poured it all out, as I was walking off, a group of media were there. Sam Donaldson ran up to me, jammed a microphone in my face, and said, "Robert Redford, who do you think is better-looking, you or Dan Quayle?" So, I'm not going to delude myself on about the impact of anything I might have to say. But my concerns, I believe, are your concerns, and they're certainly concerns that are serious enough to talk about and to share.

As I understand it, one of the things that makes this a very interesting school experience is that most of you are not just starting out, you're not just making that step into life, but you're already there, mid-career, well on your way, starting families, raising children. If that's the case, it puts an even greater emphasis on you and what role you're going to be playing in our future.

I'm sure you all feel like I do, that there is sort of an underlying chaos to daily life, and maybe it has something to do with the approaching millennium. I don't know. It would be interesting for me to look from a historical point of view at the last five years of the last century and see if there was this sort of crazed hysteria overtaking the country. Maybe it's always been this way before the turn of a century. But somehow it feels like our lives are not as free as they used to be.

We've heard a lot of slogans about things like family values, community, freedom. Very, very valuable words. Very important words to American life that are kicked around in the form of slogans for political effect. But we have to ask ourselves, I think, "Really how strong is our bond as a people and really how free are we?"

I believe that freedom comes with the ability to get a good education and a decent job. It comes with a competitive marketplace, decent training, personal safety, and a healthy environment. Now think about the freedom that comes with having a good education and a good job, the freedom that comes with being able to send a kid off to school in the morning and know that they're actually going to get there or get home. Think about the freedom that comes with fishing or swimming in a river without worrying if you're going to end up sick from pollution, or taking a deep breath outside that energizes rather than chokes.

And then there's the arts, and of course I speak probably more purely from the arts because that's my profession— that's my life. The thing about art that I think is important is that art is the freedom to choose. If you don't like it, you have the freedom not to look at it, not to buy it or to turn it off. But we have the freedom of choice to do so. If we take that choice away by law, as Jesse Helms and others like him would suggest or would like, then what we do is we take away a basic freedom, and I don't need to tell you where that will lead.

They try to justify their attempt to take away our right to free expression by calling art immoral, dangerous, or obscene. As we look at it, we say, "Well, what about it? Is it really obscene?" What's really more obscene, kids all across the country dodging bullets on the way to a school providing miserable education, or a painting? What's more obscene, Gordon Liddy telling his radio audience where to aim a bullet in order to kill, or a play involving an alternative lifestyle? Tons of toxic waste pouring into our air and water, or a rap song?

Another word we hear tossed around a lot today is "community," the bond between people and how important that is. Yet look at how hard it is to find the proverbial *us* in the national dialogue that's going on today. The only place we find it, really, is in *us versus them*.

And there is a recklessness to the rhetoric today that seems to have spun out of control. Sure, I know muckraking has been part of our society since its beginning, but what makes it different today is the sheer vacuum when it comes to real leaders and role models to balance it. Today it just seems like a low-road free-for-all, and it's getting a little spooky out there. Instead of legitimate discourses and discussion, we hear name-calling and mean-spirited personal attacks with little regard for its impact. People are being labeled as traitors and subversives, and their views as antifamily, immoral, even un-American. Things like art education and our natural resources have been rhetorical punching bags, and the serious, considered solutions we seek get lost in the flood of political spin. Our national leaders are acting like a bunch of tabloid TV reporters and not solving problems or nurturing any sense of community.

It feels to me like we're actually on some kind of brink here. Of course America's always had this sort of weird and idiosyncratic nature to pull itself from the fire right at the brink. We can look back in history and find moments where we were threatened with losing valuable constitutional rights like First Amendment rights. We can look at McCarthyism, we can look at Vietnam or Watergate. In each of these cases our rights were seriously threatened.

Maybe, maybe we're in another one of these phases today. I've heard this cry from this new generation that's coming on, that there's a dispirit about the future because opportunity and jobs have been robbed by the greedy generation that came before. Now that complaint may be so, but it's not an answer.

I still have genuine hope for the future because my hope is not, at the moment anyway, with the leadership in this country; it's with you. We're right at a point where hope, though, can't stand alone. Hope is not a solution; hope has to be joined by action.

Let's face it—leadership hasn't come from the top for a long time, and it certainly doesn't appear to be there at the moment. Because of this, all people across America are beginning to take issues into their own hands in finding answers for what threatens their communities. But there's not enough of it yet, and the collective voice isn't loud enough yet. But it can be.

Grass roots activism has produced some of the greatest achievements of the American democracy: women's suffrage, labor laws, the civil rights movement, the end of the Vietnam War, Earth Day. Real change rests with an informed and active citizenry. It rests with us. It's the best club we have to force the leadership in the country to find the courage to make thoughtful and tough decisions that need to be made.

I think we have to make it really a political liability for our elected leaders to decimate public education, poison our air and water, jeopardize the health and safety of children, infringe on our right to creative expression. Otherwise forget it. Nothing is going to change. We have to make it a political liability for our elected leaders to insist on low-road, divisive rhetoric over thoughtful, truthful discourse. Otherwise it's just going to remain with us.

It's time to turn up the heat and send a loud message that can't be ignored. It's the only way we're going to bring about the kind of changes that we want in our society. We should never forget that those in political power are merely guardians of the public trust. They don't own it, we do. It's yours, and I wish you well.

Stephen Breyer

Stanford University
June 15, 1997

*In 1994 Stephen Breyer became a member of the Supreme
Court, the ultimate reward for a distinguished legal career. A
San Francisco native and a graduate of Stanford in 1959,
Justice Breyer delivered his address the day his son, Michael,
graduated from Stanford. While he calls his speech
"traditional," his mix of humor and keen insight on democracy
are anything but routine.*

It is a particular pleasure for me to speak at your commencement because my son, Michael, is graduating—and on Father's Day too. I think I can speak for all the fathers and
mothers here in telling you that however nostalgic we are
about the children that you once were, we love and admire
the adults you have become. And we are deeply proud of
your achievements.

The *Stanford Daily* asked Michael how he felt about my
speaking. "That's fine," he said. "He's been giving me advice
for more than twenty years; I suppose another fifteen minutes
won't matter." Let me spend those fifteen minutes making a
most traditional commencement speech: a few personal remarks, the inevitable two or three minutes of free advice, and
then a prediction (or at least a hope).

This morning I gave Michael a Stanford ring—a silver ring
with an effigy of El Palo Alto—the tall tree—at its center.
As I did so I thought of my father, for it was his ring, given

him on his graduation seventy years ago. Yesterday I walked through the Inner Quad and saw the three paving stones that mark my family's three graduations: my father's graduation, my own in 1959, and yours, Michael, now. This was an emotional moment.

I thought about my father's life—growing up on Fourteenth Avenue in San Francisco, working for the School Department for forty years—and my own early life in California. I thought a little about the enormous economic change that has taken place from the railroads that initially made possible Leland Stanford's founding of this university to the Silicon Valley of today. But I realized that there have been more than economic changes and many of them for the better.

My early childhood, for example, includes memories of World War Two and of the relative, a Holocaust refugee who came from Germany through Shanghai, to live with us during the war. For my generation, "the war" means not Korea or Vietnam or the Cold War, but World War II. Consider too that when my father was at Stanford, he could not join any of the social organizations because he was Jewish, and those organizations at that time did not accept Jews. Indeed I can remember, as a child, my mother thinking of going to lunch at a downtown San Francisco hotel with a friend of hers, who was African American, and their discussing whether they would be served. When my colleagues Justices Sandra Day O'Connor and Ruth Bader Ginsburg graduated from law school, they had trouble finding jobs— because they were women. So did Senator [Dianne] Feinstein. The world has changed. Often for the better. I think it is very important to remember that those changes did not occur magically, that they represented individual, and collective, pioneering efforts. We need to remember those efforts both because so many of us now benefit from them and because there is so much still to be done. You still can choose to be a pioneer.

This brings me to a more difficult matter—a word of advice, as you try to decide "what next?" Your hearing what advantages your fine education has given you, while true, will not help you with those decisions. When I graduated, we received lots of advice: "Join the Army." "Give Blood." "Travel East." "Stay West." "The future is plastics." Have you seen *The Graduate*? There is always the risk that advice reflects the tunnel vision of one's own career. Supposedly someone asked Conrad Hilton what he might pass on to others after fifty years in the hotel business, and he replied, "Always keep the shower curtain inside the bathtub."

And of course you will be advised to ask many questions. In your careers the science graduate will ask, "Why does that work?"; the engineering graduate, "How does it work?"; the economics graduate, "What does it cost?"; and the liberal arts graduate, "Do you want french fries with that hamburger?"

But some advice rings true. Bayless Manning, former dean of Stanford Law School, pointed out to me once that when we make an important personal decision, we rarely know more than 10 percent of all we would like to know about it, let alone about the other options that the decision precludes.

Sometimes agonizing does not help; sometimes we must simply choose. And our lives then shape themselves around the choices that we make.

I take to heart an essay I once read about *Jane Eyre*. We look out, says the essayist, over any large city, and we are tempted to think that the lives within it are depressingly similar; but Charlotte Brontë's story of a governess reminds us that that is not so. It tells us that every person's life is a story of passion, with its moments of joy and happiness, of tragedy or sorrow. And each person's story is different, one from the other.

The external circumstances, the material circumstances, of that story are often beyond our control, but they often matter less than we think. We all know many people who complain despite having a glass full to overflowing. And my wife, who works with children at Dana Farber Cancer Institute, sees many families who bring joy to others and to themselves by seeing a glass half full that others see half empty.

The most important parts of the story are the personal parts as, through our choices, we create the story. Your story will include friends and family, not just career. And at times it will call upon you to participate in the life of the community in which you live and to help those who are less fortunate.

Most important, our stories include our own justifications for our actions and our motives—in light of our own values. We cannot escape the negative meaning that a failure of integrity—a failure to live up to our own basic standards of right and wrong—will give to the story that throughout our lives we tell ourselves. I agree with the philosopher who said that money can vanish overnight, power disappear, even that bubble reputation can evaporate, but character—personal integrity—is a rock that is secure and that no one can take from you.

Now, may I make a prediction? Certainly predictions are dangerous, which is why Casey Stengel said, "I never make predictions—at least not about the future." But if mine proves wrong, I am in good company. Consider: 1895: The president of the British Royal Society predicts, "Heavier than air flying machines are impossible." 1899: The chief of the U.S. Patent Office announces, "Everything that can be invented has been invented." 1927: The head of Warner Brothers asks, "Who . . . wants to hear actors talk?" 1943: Tom Watson, the president of IBM, announces, "I think there is a world market for maybe five computers." 1949: *Popular Mechanics* points out, "Computers in the future may weigh no more than 1.5 tons." 1981: Bill Gates admonishes, "640K ought to be enough for anyone."

What is it that one can predict with any certainty at all about the world in which your grandchildren will graduate? Daniel Bell has predicted—and he thought it fairly obvious— that one hundred years from now we will have recently inaugurated a President of the United States, following a free election the preceding November. I share that prediction and hope. It sounds unremarkable, yet that very fact—that it is unremarkable—suggests something unique about our society. And our prediction tells us something about our nation—its past, present, and future—and about your place within it.

With respect to the past, Bell's prediction tells us that democratic institutions, our Constitution, government, and laws, are not simply words on paper but are principles that have claimed the allegiance of generations. To see this, consider *Brown* v. *Board of Education*, the case that ended legal segregation by race. *Brown* provides an example of law at its best, working to include among us groups that were previously excluded. When a Russian general recently asked me how the judges, through *Brown* and later cases, succeeded in ending legal segregation in America, I replied that it was not simply the judges, for neither nine Supreme Court justices, nor nine hundred judges nor nine thousand judges, could themselves have ended segregation. I told the Russian general about the Supreme Court's order to integrate the schools of Arkansas when its governor stood in the schoolhouse door and said no. I told him that the President of the United States ordered American troops to Arkansas. Only then did the black children enter the white school. And that presidential decision reflects not words on paper or judicial decisions but history and custom and a tradition that we built after suffering a terrible civil war. It reflected too the understanding that a country with so many different groups of people, of so many different religions and races and backgrounds, can best solve its differences not through wars but through respect for law.

That is the point. The carrying out of our commitment as a nation to basic principles of democracy, liberty, and fairness has depended upon custom, tradition, and commitment to the enterprise, not just by politicians and judges but by millions of ordinary citizens. I experience the working of that tradition every day in my job. My parents' generation passed on that tradition to mine; we must to yours; and you must to your children. Otherwise our society and our law—however decent and fair in principle—will not work in practice.

And so I come to the present. Bell's prediction about the durability of our democratic institutions reminds us of an important feature of the Constitution. That document in fact tells us how to solve very few of our nation's problems. It is an enabling (and constraining) document. Part of it describes a mechanism for making and applying law, creating a framework for representative government. Part protects our basic freedoms, permitting us to exercise our rights to speak freely, to worship freely, and to choose our nation's course peacefully and democratically. Part protects the basic fairness of our system, so that majorities cannot unfairly and systematically oppress minorities. As a whole the Constitution gives us the freedom to choose; it does not tell us what to choose. Rather it forces us, as a community, to choose democratically how we will solve our nation's problems. It therefore requires our participation, for without that our Constitution and our country cannot work.

As to the future, Bell's prediction expresses a hope. It is the hope that you will participate in the affairs of your communities and your nation. Some would say that today's challenges are less clear—that, unlike my father's generation, you

new form of
violence

face no Hitler, no Nazis abroad; that unlike mine, you need not confront the evil of legal segregation by race. But you do face inner cities where the greatest threat to children's lives is homicide; where drugs and crime are prevalent but education, jobs, and hope are scarce. You do face the ever-shrinking world, with its growing populations and rapid development, with threats of terrorism and ethnic wars. You do face the cutting down of forests, the heating up of climate, the overfishing of the sea, which threaten our earth's environment. You do face the challenge of building a multiracial society. The challenges are there. And they are clear.

Some say that our governmental institutions are failing us. Many are cynical; public confidence in government is at an all-time low. But I see this as just one more challenge. If you do not trust the way our government works, make it work better. Government, after all, is no more than its individual citizens, showing their "public face," working together to solve the joint problems that we share as a community. Cynicism does not help.

Some say that moral confusion is becoming a great and insurmountable obstacle to a healthy, flourishing society, that television, movies, and the press have somehow confused us, so that we have lost our moral compass. I do not believe that can be so. Society changes; notions of right and wrong may change to a degree, but only at the edges. We do know right from wrong; you do know right from wrong. Personal integrity—that rock—at the core remains the same.

Some say that you are too concerned about economic opportunities to have time for community affairs—though your record of volunteer activities belies this. Indeed I trust you will confront and overcome pressures and problems that my generation did not have to face or did not succeed in overcoming. But our nation has never had so much influence in the world, Stanford graduates—even the liberal arts graduates—have never faced such a range of opportunities, and the future offers you greater possibilities and greater challenges than to any prior generation.

So I think that Bell's prediction, and mine, our hope, will come to pass. And your lives will tell stories that have not just a private, personal part but a public, a community part as well. Justice Holmes at a commencement many years ago said, "That, as life is action and passion, it is required of a man that he should share the passion and action of his time at peril of being judged not to have lived." That is a better charge to each man and woman here than any I could write. I urge you to follow that advice. I greatly congratulate the Stanford Class of 1997. And I wish each of you a life of passion, action, integrity, participation—a long and most fulfilling story.

Mario Cuomo

Iona College
June 3, 1984

*Mario Cuomo served as the governor of New York from 1983
to 1994. One of the most recognized political figures in the
nation, Cuomo has often been suggested as a possible
presidential candidate, although he has never run for the office.
In this speech, Cuomo takes the unusual step of addressing the
parents of the graduates.*

It was an Irishman who gave me the best advice I've ever
been given about the art of delivering a commencement
speech.

Father Flynn was the president of my alma mater, St.
John's, and the first time I was ever asked to speak at a
graduation, I asked him how I should approach it.

"Commencement speakers," said Father Flynn, "should
think of themselves as the body at an old-fashioned Irish
wake. They need you in order to have the party, but nobody
expects you to say very much."

That's advice I intend to remember today. . . .

I know that you are thinking—good parents and grandparents, loved ones of the graduates—what I'm thinking.
"We've been through it all, at least most of it, or a lot of it.
There's so much ahead that they ought to know about. So
many temptations they should ignore. So much we can tell
them about how to begin answering these hard questions."

We have the obligation to tell them, to reduce as much as

possible the pain of their learning only from their own blunders.

We have the obligation. But do we have the right?

Can we, who found the ultimate truth so elusive for so long, tell them with confidence now of the futility of gathering up riches and the things of the world?

It's clear to us that all the newly won power over space and time, the conquest of the forces of nature, the fulfilling of age-old challenges, have not made us any happier or surer of ourselves.

We have built rockets and spaceships and shuttles; we have harnessed the atom; we have dazzled a generation with a display of our technological skills. But we still spend millions of dollars on aspirin and psychiatrists and tissues to wipe away the tears of anguish and uncertainty that result from our confusion and our emptiness.

Most of us have achieved levels of affluence and comfort unthought of two generations ago.

We've never had it so good, most of us.

Nor have we ever complained so bitterly about our problems.

The closed circle of pure materialism is clear to us now— aspirations become wants, wants become needs, and self-gratification becomes a bottomless pit.

All around us we have seen success in this world's terms become ultimate and desperate failure. Teenagers and college students, raised in affluent surroundings and given all the material comforts our society can offer, commit suicide.

Entertainers and sports figures achieve fame and wealth but find the world empty and dull without the solace or stimulation of drugs.

Men and women rise to the top of their professions after years of struggling. But despite their apparent success, they are driven nearly mad by a frantic search for diversions, new mates, games, new experiences—anything to fill the diminishing interval between their existence and eternity.

We know because we've been there. But do we have the right to tell these graduates that the most important thing in their lives will be their ability to believe in believing? And that without that ability, sooner or later they will be doomed to despair?

Do you think they would believe us if we told them today what we know to be true: that after the pride of obtaining a degree and maybe later another degree and after their first few love affairs, that after earning their first big title, their first shiny new car, and traveling around the world for the first time and having had it all, they will discover that none of it counts unless they have something real and permanent to believe in?

Tell me, ladies and gentlemen, are we the ones to tell them what their instructors have tried to teach them for years?

That the philosophers were right. That Saint Francis, Buddha, Muhammad, Maimonides—all spoke the truth when they said the way to serve yourself is to serve others; and that Aristotle was right, before them, when he said the only way to assure yourself happiness is to learn to give happiness.

Don't you remember that we were told all this when we were younger? But nevertheless, we got caught up in the struggle and the sweat and the frustration and the joy of small victories and forgot it all. Until recently, when we began to look back.

How simple it seems now. We thought the Sermon on the Mount was a nice allegory and nothing more. What we didn't understand until we got to be a little older was that it was the whole answer, the whole truth. That the way—the only way—to succeed and to be happy is to learn those rules so basic that a shepherd's son could teach them to an ignorant flock without notes or formulae.

We carried Saint Francis's prayer in our wallets for years and never learned to live the message.

Do we have the right now to tell them that when Saint Francis begged the Lord to teach him to want to console instead of seeking to be consoled—to teach him to want to love instead of desiring to be loved—that he was really being intensely selfish? Because he knew the only way to be fulfilled and pleased and happy was to give instead of trying to get.

We have for a full lifetime taught our children to be go-getters. Can we now say to them that if they want to be happy, they must be go-givers?

I wonder if we can, in good conscience, say these things to them today, when we ourselves failed so often to practice what we would preach.

I wonder if we—who have fought, argued, and bickered and so often done the wrong thing to one another—are the ones to teach them love.

How do we tell them that one ought not to be discouraged by imperfection in the world and the inevitability of death and diminishment? How do we tell them when they lose a child, or are crippled, or know that they will themselves die soon that God permits pain and sickness and unfairness and evil to exist only in order to permit us to test our mettle and to earn a fulfillment that would otherwise not be possible?

How can we tell our children that, when we have ourselves so often cried out in bitter despair at what we regarded to be the injustice of life and when we have so often surrendered?

How can we tell them that it is their duty to use all that they have been given to make a better world, not only for themselves and their families but for all who live in this world, when it was our generation that made the world a place where the great powers are so alienated from one another that they can't even play together in an Olympics?

Do we have the right to tell them, as our teachers told us,

that they have an obligation in justice to participate in politics and government? Can we without shame say to them that our system of democracy works well only when there is involvement by all? That in our democracy the policies that become law, the rules of justice, the treatment of individuals are the responsibility of each citizen? That you get what you deserve out of our system and that indifference deserves nothing good?

When we ourselves have chosen to sit at home on so many election days, muttering grim remarks about the politicians who appear on the television set, instead of doing what we could to change things for the better?

Will they believe us if we said these things?

Would we be able to explain the embarrassment of our own failures?

Do you blame me, ladies and gentlemen, for being reluctant to deliver to them the message that is traditional on commencement day?

But maybe, ladies and gentlemen, this problem is not as great as I've made it out to be.

I've been taking a close look at these graduates. They are actually taller, stronger, smarter than we were, smart enough maybe to take our mistakes as their messages, to make our weaknesses their lessons, and to make our example—good and not so good—part of their education.

I think I see in their eyes a depth of perception that perhaps we didn't have. A sense of truth, deeper and less fragile than ours.

As you talk to them, you get the feeling that they are certainly mature enough to see the real problems of our society: the need for peace, the need to keep pure the environment God offered us, the need to provide people the dignity of earning their own way.

Indeed, as I think about it, I have to conclude that these

young people before me today are the best reason for hope that this world knows.

I see them as believers and doers who will take what we will pass on to them so clumsily and make it something better than we have ever known. Honoring us by their works, but wanting to be better than we have been.

I tell you, ladies and gentlemen, looking at them now, closer and harder than I have before, I have a feeling about these people that makes me want to live long enough to see and be part of the world they will create.

Now, ladies and gentlemen, parents and grandparents, I would like to tell them, the graduates, all of this, and I know that if we thought they wouldn't be embarrassed by hearing it, we would all be telling them about how proud we are of them and how much we believe in them and their future. But again maybe we don't have to tell them; maybe they know. Maybe they can tell us just by seeing the love in our eyes today.

Congratulations, ladies and gentlemen, on the good children you have cared for and raised.

Ann Richards

Mount Holyoke College
May 28, 1995

*Former Governor of Texas Ann Richards gained national
recognition when, in 1992, she roused the Democratic National
Convention with her speech nominating Bill Clinton for the
presidency. She's remained a colorful and inspiring figure on
the national political landscape ever since. She delivered this
address at Mount Holyoke, where she received an honorary
degree in Law.*

When I was invited to be a part of this commencement, I
knew that the distinguishing characteristic of Mount Holyoke
was that the students here are given a firm indocrination and
a drive in public service. My friend Jane Hickie,* Class of
1970, and I have shared about twenty years of that drive in
the fast lane of Texas politics. And I would like all of you
to know that she's represented you well in Texas and in
Washington, D.C. When their twenty-fifth college reunion
approaches, most people get new wardrobes or they rent ex-
pensive cars or visit the plastic surgeon for one last skirmish,
trying to deal with the war against gravity. Jane has to make
do with bringing along her old friend, who is terrifically flat-
tered by your invitation and degree. I told my friends at home
they now had to call me Dr. Governor! It is wonderful to

*Jane Hickie was the director of the Texas Office of State-Federal Relations during
Richards's tenure as governor.

get a doctorate of Laws. I was married to a lawyer for thirty years, so I earned it.

Someone asked me to begin by giving you some insight into the unique nature of the Texas political environment. Well, let me put it this way. I come from a short line of women governors. The only other woman governor of Texas was Miriam Amanda Ferguson. She was called Ma Ferguson because she was married to Pa Ferguson. Anyway, she ran a couple of times. She was initially elected governor because Pa had been impeached.*

I was born the same year she took office the last time she was elected. But what's important for me to tell you about Ma was her gaining undying notoriety when there was a big issue in Texas and that was whether or not children were going to be punished for speaking Spanish in public schools. When Ma was asked what she thought about the issue, she said, "If the English language was good enough for Jesus Christ, it was good enough for the schoolchildren of Texas." I tell you that so you know that we have learned something and made some progress in Texas in the last fifty or so years.

Just a few months after I was elected, you can imagine what it's like. There's a great deal of turmoil going on, the legislature was already in session, the issues were already hot and heavy, I was trying to assemble a staff, plan an inauguration with all of the attendant balls and marches, and we received word that the queen of England was coming to visit Texas. And I don't know how many of you have entertained the queen, but it's a very complicated deal. We all had to go to school to learn not to touch the elbow and things like that. I had to go have a dress made. One of those sort of suitable,

---

*Miriam Amanda Ferguson was governor of Texas from 1924 to 1926. Indeed, her husband, James E. Ferguson, governor of Texas from 1915 to 1917, was impeached in 1917.

queenly-looking outfits with the silk pleated skirt and the raw silk jacket and bright color. After all of this preparation, obviously we were nervous and wanted the visit to go very well. I was running across the rotunda of the Capitol building to wait there on the front steps for the queen and Prince Philip, and racing through my mind came my mother's voice, just as clear as a bell, saying "Where do you think you're going, to see the queen of England?" Here some forty years later I was!

At the conclusion of the queen's visit, after she had gone to a number of Texas cities, there was a dinner in Houston that was hosted by the queen and Prince Philip to repay the gestures we had extended to them on their visit. They had invited all of the mayors of the cities that they had visited. There we all were in our finery standing at the receiving line. At one end was the mayor of Houston, Kathy Whitmeyer, then the queen and Prince Philip, then here I am. These mayors start coming through the receiving line, mayor of Dallas, the mayor of San Antonio, of Corpus Christi, of Galveston, of San Marcos—and they were all women!

Prince Philip turned and looked at me and looked at them, and then he said to the queen, "I say it looks rather like a matriarchy," and without batting an eye the queen said, "I think that's rather nice, don't you?" Despite the queen's good wishes, Texas is nowhere near a state of matriarchy, which is fine because matriarchy is not what we are all after. We have learned that when the scales are weighted in favor of one gender or one race or one privileged background, no one in society is well served.

When my grandmother was a girl, according to Texas law, the only people who could not vote were idiots, imbeciles, the insane, and women. And of course the idea of minority voting—at least without directed supervision—was beyond the pale. Before the mid-1950s women could not serve on juries. And it surprises a lot of young women to learn that there were places in this country where we could not get credit in our own names until the the mid-1970s. I was working for a young woman I had helped to elect to the Texas legislature, Sarah Waddington, who argued the *Roe* v. *Wade* case before the Supreme Court, and Sarah and I worked very hard on a bill that would allow women to get credit, because at that time you could be earning your own living, but if you wanted a loan, you had to take your brother or your father or your husband or someone suitable, respectable, and male to go down to the bank with you and vouch for you. I saw something in *Newsweek* the other day about Hillary Clinton's visit to the Far East and to India and about the Grameen rural bank that lends money to poor people in developing nations to help them start businesses. They have actually begun giving preferences to women when they make loans because the payback rate is better. And while the men tended to spend the money they made on themselves, women spent it on children and their business. They said at the bank that the social benefits were simply much greater when women got the money. Which is a conclusion I am delighted to promote and one that proves that if we are given the opportunity, indeed we can perform and perform well.

Now, truly that is all we have ever been after, an honest chance to show what we can do. It should not come as a surprise that when I began my involvement in politics, women made the coffee, and men made the decisions. But with more of us running for and winning public office, we are seeing fundamental changes in the public perception of women in public service. We are at an awkward and rather wonderful stage where people invest us with remarkable attributes. They believe we are more honest and less likely to protect the status quo, and they are more ready than ever to vote for us.

I can still remember a time when constituents might get us off in a little corner for a little quiet chitchat and inquire if we hated our father or something. For after all, why else would we want this man's job? The great majority of us— men and women—I hope have gotten beyond this point. As more of us hold public office, we're finding out that we are human after all, that we have our attributes and we have our shortcomings.

But we are still a long way from that complete equality and full participation that has been our goal for generations. All the studies and polls show that many people share the viewpoint of one of Lily Tomlin's characters in *The Search for Signs of Intelligent Life in the Universe*. That no matter how cynical you become, it's never enough to keep up. And that applies to government more than most institutions. For all of you sitting there, with your sunflowers, your mortarboards, I hope you will not give in to cynicism. Now that men have learned to make coffee and a few women are in decision-making positions, it would be a calamity to turn away just when we can make the most difference. Just when we can be the difference between a system that collapses under its own tired weight and a system that is rejuvenated by fresh faces, fresh voices, and fresh ideas.

It is not that women are better than men. But I long ago accepted and I hope that you realize we are different. The most sympathetic and sensitive of our men friends cannot, no matter how hard they try, hear with a woman's ear or process information through a woman's experience. This should not be any great revelation for any of us. Hispanics, African Americans, Asian Americans, minorities have patiently and usually with uncommon gentleness tried to explain for years to Anglos those issues seen differently from inside a black or a brown skin than for those of us who are white.

The experience is different. The perspective is different.

The knowing is different. We see it many ways in our society now, and I see it often in policy deliberations. A debate about funding for mental retardation facilities is changed tremendously by the presence of a parent of a child with Down's syndrome. Because the knowing and the understanding is different from a firsthand experience. A dialogue about equal opportunity takes on new meaning. Because the knowing and the understanding is different from a firsthand experience. A dialogue about equal opportunity takes on new meaning and it takes on immediacy when a person of color is sitting in that room. A question of health care is enhanced by the presence of someone who has reached their majority years and is concerned about a future that will perhaps not include the very best of care.

When I am in a meeting and the subject is affirmative action or local government or the public schools, the nature of the discussion changes because I am a woman, a former county commissioner, a former schoolteacher. The analogies are endless, but the point is always the same. When you add someone whose understanding is not intellectual, but instinctive, the whole equation and the whole understanding changes.

Now I am not suggesting to you that we are needed in the corridors of power because we will make a difference about stereotypical women's issues like sexual harassment or parental leave. Nor am I suggesting to you that women are the only ones qualified to deal with those issues. What I am saying is that because our background is different, we pick up different nuances and bring valuable skills to the process. And we bring along the viewpoints of half the population of the United States of America.

The real question for women, and I think, minorities, for all of us who have been excluded in the past, whose noses are flat from peering in through that glass window, is: What changes will our participation in public service cause? Virginia Woolf wrote: "There they go—our brothers—mounting those steps, passing in and out of those doors, ascending those pulpits . . . preaching, teaching, administering justice, making money. A procession is always a solemn sight. And there traipsing along the tail end, we go. And that makes a difference. We too can lead the House [of Commons], can mount those steps and pass in and out of those halls, administer justice, make money. But we must ask ourselves, on what terms will we join the procession?" Virginia Woolf wrote that at a time when it was not at all certain that women would join the procession, when we were watching the show from a discreet Victorian distance.

In an incredibly short time we have moved from watching at the end of the procession, and now, we move, with our brothers, to the head of the procession and into leadership. And what might Virginia Woolf ask are our terms? Of the procession, we ask that our perspective as women be valued. But of ourselves, we ask more: that our participation makes our society more just, makes it more humane, makes our government more determined to meet the needs of all the human beings who live in it. Last evening I had a wonderful dinner with many of the professors from the government department. Jean Grossholtz raised the question: "What commitment will we make to build a community rather than divide it?"

I think that what you see today that comes into your living rooms on television doesn't suggest builders in Washington. It suggests people who are divisive. And so I am saying to you as you go from these hallowed halls and enter into positions of leadership in public service . . . I think what Mary Lyon* conceived at Mount Holyoke was to prepare you for

---

*Mary Lyon founded Mount Holyoke in 1837.

leadership that unites, not wrests apart. I think that the education that you have received here has focused you to understand that there are those out there who have not had the privilege of being in these hallowed halls and who desperately need you to help them. Particularly children and particularly the elderly. Don't get caught up in the political rhetoric; live with the reality of service. Please understand that when you hear rhetorical reference today to those who are on welfare with the suggestion that they do not deserve it, what they are really talking about are your fathers and mothers and mine, who are going to be turned away from health care, not welfare.

And so, my friends, it is not matriarchy we are after. It is something far more important. And when the struggle seems long and difficult, it might be useful to remember what Thurgood Marshall told us: that it is not only how far we have come but how close we are. Your role in shaping public policy is vital to our future. Now as you set off on that drive, I thought the least I could do is to offer a little personal advice to you. Now that the preaching is over, I thought I should give you five rules for living that have worked for me.

The first rule in life is: Cherish your friends and family as if your life depended on it. Because it does.

Number two: Love people more than things. You know those T-shirts that say "He who dies with the most toys wins." I'm going to promise you that over the years I've spent my life collecting a great number of things I thought I would die without. And I wouldn't give you a nickel for most of it today.

Number three: Indulge the fool in you. Encourage the clown and the laughter that is inside of you. Go ahead and do it! Make time for play, for the impractical, for the absurd, and make it a rule to do it. Not just every now and then. Let your heart overrule your head once in a while. Never turn down a new experience unless it's against the law or will get you in serious trouble.

Number four: Don't spend a lot of time worrying about your failures. I've learned a whole lot more from my mistakes than from all my successes.

And number five: Have some sense about work. No one ever died muttering, "I wish I spent more time at the office."

There is a wonderful world out there. It's just waiting for your energy and your ideas. We need you.

God bless you and Godspeed.

Alice Walker

Agnes Scott College
May 17, 1997

Alice Walker is one of America's most respected and outspoken writers and poets. Author of many works, she is best known for her 1982 novel The Color Purple, *which won the Pulitzer Prize and the American Book Award. In this address at Agnes Scott College, Walker contrasts the miracle of birth with the problems of bringing children into a troubled world.*

Last year, December 17 at seven-sixteen in the morning, to be exact, I witnessed my first birth. To see a baby being born was something I have always wanted to do since I myself was a child and first heard the mysterious information that babies came out of women's bodies.

I had been invited to this birth by the midwife, who is a friend of mine, and also by the mother and grandmother of the baby involved.

I arrived at the birth mother's home in the early dawn—the exact time, it seems to me, that one should be summoned. Four o'clock in the morning, if I recall correctly. As I mounted the steps leading to the mother's door, I heard her cries.

This seemed as it should be. I clearly felt—the world being as populated as it is with human beings—that I should have been hearing these cries before. The living room as I entered it, having removed my shoes at the entrance, also seemed ancient, even cavelike, as friends of the young mother sat about in clusters, quietly talking, or made tea and coffee for those just entering.

I was asked by my midwife friend to hold the light, and as labor progressed, I was privileged to see each of its many stages. Every aspect of it filled me with awe. Until the last moment I could not bring myself to believe a baby would be the result of what I was seeing. The young mother was oblivious to all but her pain, those of us helping her so attuned to her feelings that during contractions we instinctively panted and breathed with her.

Four hours after my arrival the baby dropped out of his mother into the soft palm of my midwife friend. And in one fluid motion she laid him on his mother's breast. It was a remarkably beautiful birth. And the mother, only sixteen years old, had demonstrated an authority and courage that were pure warriorship.

As the birth of the baby was announced outside the bedroom in which it had occurred, the men of the tribe—the baby was born into an extended Native American family—quietly began to make breakfast, which they served to the women who had participated in the birthing and later to the clan of people who gathered to celebrate the birth throughout the day. I left this experience feeling blessed, inspired, somehow purified.

The next baby I encountered was in Careyes, Mexico, where I have a home and where I sometimes go to write. As a near, quickly reached third-world country, Mexico is ideal for me because it offers a constant reminder of all that is transpiring in over two thirds of the so-called developing world. This little girl was six months old when we met. I feel for her instantly. Perhaps it was the elegant baldness of her head. Her direct, curious gaze. Her scent of happiness. Not since my own daughter was born many years ago had I felt such joy as I beheld in a new addition to our world.

Her parents are Mexican and Italian and quite well off, and so she has a nurse and a nursery, her own pristine wing, located in her parents' spectacular sea cliff house. She has excellent food, beautiful, tiny dresses, and piles of toys. She will be raised to be upper class. This of course worries me.

It worries me partly because of the third baby I encountered during this same period. This was the six-week-old daughter of the Mexican woman who keeps house for me, a struggling middle-aged, single mother of three who recently married a man who convinced her to try to give him a son. On my way to visit her and to bring gifts for the baby and mother, I pondered the baby's future. The house into which she was born is as different from the previous house as could be imagined. Essentially one long room, with what appeared to be a dirt floor, in part of a crumbling building that rises very close to a noisy road.

The furniture in the house consisted of one bed, a table, and a couple of chairs. When the mother went to get the baby for me to see, it was as if she rummaged among a pile of rags on the bed before fetching her up. Which she did, quite proudly. Though after talking with her for a while, it became clear that her marriage was troubled and that her body was not healing properly from the birth. I urged her to return to the hospital, noting not only her own lack of energy but that the child seemed languid as well.

What will be the fate of these three children? And why should the graduating class of Agnes Scott College care?

The first child's mother is too young and unskilled to take on the task of raising a child. Fortunately the child's grandmother is present, as is the native community into which he was born. This child will have many challenges, as an Indian, in a world in which much of what might have gone into strengthening him has deliberately been, by the dominant culture, destroyed. His primary obstacle in life might well be despair. On the other hand, he enters a community that is conscious of what it is, what its struggle to survive is, and also what its commitment to its own values must be. It is also a community that truly venerates beauty, justice, and love.

The second baby's parents, it seemed to me—with their baby's spotless white nursery wing in a very casual, poor, and colorful Mexico—are attempting to seal her off from the raw poverty that exists less than ten minutes away. And I dread the day when she will awaken to her overwhelming class privilege, in a country whose children, generally speaking, have so little. I dread even more, however, the possibility that by the time she is an adult, the material disparity between herself and others will have no meaning to her. That she will walk over and around and through her nurse, the servants, and the population of poor Mexicans without seeing their condition of poverty or even really seeing them. This would be a disaster in one born so beautiful and so inspiring of love.

If I were writing a fairy tale, I would say that the little girl born across the way on the bed that resembled a pile of rags would grow up to be the servant of the rich little girl in the sea cliff castle, who is nonetheless at this stage very sweet. The little rich girl, let us name her Hope, would resist becoming the spoiled snob I fear she might become, and instead she and the poor girl, let us call her Joy, would instantly become friends of such fastness that Hope's parents would be at a loss about what to make of their devotion. Hope would quietly teach Joy everything there is to know about place settings and table manners, horseback riding and society dances. Joy would teach Hope all there is to know about cardplaying and swimming in the river and how to shop in the barrio without ever encountering a glance or word of disrespect. They would be mutually disgusted that Joy was so poor and Hope's parents so rich. They would set out to find a way to equalize things.

Along would come, perhaps, the third child, now a fully grown Native American man, a warrior, like his mother. He would join the two women. Together they would teach the children of the very poor, many of whom are indigenous. They would agitate for economic democracy in Mexico. They would be vilified as Communists in the press and chased out of town. They would take to the mountains. From there, they, along with the thousands who would come to join them, would begin the second Mexican revolution. Perhaps they would model their rebellion on the Zapatista movement, which is ongoing presently in the Mexican state of Chiapas.

But this is not a fairy tale.

What will in fact be the lives of these children? This is the cry that must wake us from our sleep.

Since you invited me here on this special day—the day in which you launch yourselves into the world—I will feel free in giving you the advantage of my own harsh opinion about having children just now. *I believe there should be a moratorium on the birth of children.* That not one more child should be born on this planet until certain conditions are met. The first of these is that the several missing pounds of plutonium— the most deadly substance ever concocted by man; the inhalation of a single particle causes cancer—must be found. I believe it was the valiant Dr. Helen Caldicott who alerted us to the fact that it is missing, just as she labored for over a decade to warn us of the lethal effects of nuclear power and nuclear waste. Where is the awful substance? Who has stolen it? To what purpose will they use it? And what about the rumor one hears of plutonium being used to fuel rockets, which, as we know, sometimes self-destruct, scattering their fuel and the bodies of their crew right over the face of mother earth.

Begin, then, with tracking the use and whereabouts of the plutonium. If we do not find it, and contain it, there is not much hope that any of our children will live free from pain into a healthy old age. And from there, work to make the routine of drinking bottled water a distant nightmare. Water was not meant to be polluted, any more than human blood is meant to be contaminated. How dare we bring anyone into the world who must, anywhere on earth, run from rain.

Next, there are the lives of the other animals—humans being only one, and a minority—to be considered. These must be honored. The lives of plants, trees in particular. These must be treated with the same respect we give our lungs.

The list, dear graduating class, is only too long. But I leave it with you, for that time in your life when you will sit quietly and thoughtfully on a secluded hill somewhere and consciously dream up a future for your very own child.

For you will have children, the majority of you. You will not listen to me at all. I myself do not listen to me. And I have to laugh as I think of this. It is such a classic predicament of human nature. For even as I enumerate the perils we face as a planet, the instability of every single system, the unresponsiveness of society, and the lethal nature of "progress," I find myself longing—hence my recent fixation on babies— to be a grandmother.

I say to my daughter more frequently than she would like, "Where is my grandchild?"

And I am not wrong in this. For I know, beyond a shadow of a doubt, that babies are by nature wonderful. And that is why so many of us want them.

My own baby's birth was a miracle from which I shall never recover. The way she felt and smelled will be forever a part of why I adore life.

What, then, does such a mixed message mean? I hear you wondering.

Well, what I've come to realize about myself is that usually what I mean about anything that I feel passionately about, when you get right down to it, is hard work. My natural home apparently sits right between a rock and a hard place. And I have had to learn to find comfort there. You can too.

So have your work in the world, and have your babies. Only one, please, out of respect for the weight we are to our mother. But be aware that the other children of the world are your responsibility as well. You must learn to see them, to feel them, as yours. Until you do, there is no way you can make your own child feel safe. And because when you do, you will join the rest of the world in cleaning up the rivers, clearing the air, saving the trees, and finding every ounce of that missing plutonium.

What happens to the three children in my non-fairy tale will be largely up to the adults of the world, people like you.

I have named the little rich girl Hope. The poor little girl Joy. I will now name the Native American boy Song. And here is a poem for them:

> On the day that you are born
> beautiful beings
> those who love you
> tremble
> We tremble because we are afraid
>
> you are so mysterious
> beautiful beings
> and we do not know
> who sent you
> nor do we know
> where you are from
>
> Imagine how perplexed
> you make us
> as your bald head

slides gracefully
into view
between your mother's
thighs
and we hold our breaths
as, after so much pain to her, you casually
drop.

What struggles you have already
endured
just
to get here!
How come we could not
welcome you
in awe?

Watching you emerge
into the light
we wonder if what we see
is even possible
If we were religious
we would cross
ourselves.

And remembering that the cross
symbolizes that place
where spirit and matter
meet
we might cross ourselves
anyway
out of the respect
for the crossroad
your birth
presents
for your mother
and you.

Oh, little ones
who will one day
be
so much taller than us
let us pledge
on your bald heads
to make a better show
of things
than we have done.

Let us promise
to take courage
from the mysterious
nature of your
journey.

Let us acknowledge
in all humility
that regardless of
your status in life
it is we
who are blessed.

We do not know the beginning
or the end
we only see the middle of things
which is our own life

Perhaps you are a part of
the force
that is coming to help
us
rearrange our world
we pray that this is
so.

· That you have come back
to help heal the confusion
you left behind
so may lifetimes
ago.

And that you come
bringing all
we need
to get the job
done:

Joy, Hope, Song.

III

Remember the Past, Embrace the Future

We Americans seem to ignore our past. Perhaps we fear having one and burn it behind us like rocket fuel, always looking forward.

—KEN BURNS

Bill Clinton

Princeton University
June 4, 1996

President William Jefferson Clinton, the forty-second President of the United States, became in 1996 the first Democratic President to win reelection after serving a full term since Franklin Delano Roosevelt won his fourth term in 1944. By inviting Clinton to be its commencement speaker, Princeton continued its tradition of inviting a President to speak at the university every fifty years. The following is an excerpt from his address.

I would like to talk to the senior class today about not only the importance of your education, but the importance of everyone else's education to your future.

At every pivotal moment in American history, Princeton, its leadership, its students, have played a crucial role. Many of our Founding Fathers were among your first sons. A president of Princeton was the only university president to sign the Declaration of Independence. This hall was occupied by the British in 1776, liberated by Washington's army in 1777, and, as the president said, sanctified forever to American history by the deliberations of the Continental Congress in 1783.

In 19—excuse me—in 1896, the last time there was a Class of '96, when Princeton celebrated its 150th anniversary, and as has been said, Grover Cleveland was President, Professor Woodrow Wilson gave his very famous speech "Princeton in the Nation's Service." I read that speech before I came here today, and I'd like to read just a brief quote from it:

"Today we must stand as those who would count their force for the future. Those who made Princeton are dead. Those who shall keep it and better it still live; they are even ourselves."

What he said about Princeton a hundred years ago applied then to America and applies to America even more today. At the time of that speech one hundred years ago, America was living as it is living today through a period of enormous change. The industrial age brought incredible new opportunities and great new challenges to our people. Princeton, through Wilson and his contemporaries, was at the center of efforts to master these powerful forces of change in a way that would enable all Americans to benefit from them and protect our time-honored values. Less than three years after he left this campus, Woodrow Wilson became President of the United States. He followed Theodore Roosevelt as the leader of America's response to that time of change. We now know it as the Progressive Era.

Today, on the edge of a new century, all of you, our Class of '96, are living through another time of great change, standing on the threshold of a new progressive era. Powerful forces are changing forever our jobs, our neighborhoods, the institutions which shape our lives. For many Americans this is a time of enormous opportunity, but for others it's a time of profound insecurity. They wonder whether their old skills and their enduring values will be enough to keep up with the challenges of this new age.

In 1996, like 1896, we really do stand at the dawn of a profoundly new era. I have called it the Age of Possibility because of the revolution in information and technology, and market capitalism sweeping the globe, a world no longer divided by the Cold War. Just consider this, there's more computer power in a Ford Taurus every one of you can buy and drive to the supermarket than there was in *Apollo II*, when

Neil Armstrong took it to the moon. Nobody who wasn't a high-energy physicist had even heard of the World Wide Web when I became President. And now even my cat, Socks, has his own page. By the time a child born today is old enough to read, over one hundred million people will be on the Internet.

This Age of Possibility means that more Americans than ever before will be able to live out their dreams. Indeed, for all of you in the Class of '96, this Age of Possibility is actually an age of high probability, in large measure because of the excellent education you celebrate today.

But we know that not all Americans see the future that way. We know that about half of our people in this increasingly global economy are working harder and harder without making any more money, that about half of the people who lose their jobs today don't ever find another job doing as well as they were doing in the previous one.

We know that therefore, our mission today must be to ensure that all of our people have the opportunity to live out their dreams in a nation that remains the world's strongest force for peace and freedom, for prosperity, for our commitment that we can respect our diversity and still find unity.

This is about more than money. Opportunity is what defines this country. For 220 years, the idea of opportunity for all and the freedom to seize it have literally been the defining elements of America. They were always ideals, never perfectly realized, but always our history has been a steady march of striving to live up to them.

Having these ideals achievable, imaginable for all is an important part of maintaining our sense of democracy and our ability to forge an American community with such disparate elements of race and religion and ethnicity across so many borders that could so easily divide this country.

And so I say to you, creating opportunity for all, the opportunity that everyone has that many of you are now exercising, dreaming about your future, that is what you must do in order to make sure that this Age of Possibility is really that for all Americans.

When I took office, I was concerned about the uncertain steps our country was taking toward that future. We'd let our deficit get out of hand. Unemployment had exploded. Job growth was the lowest since the Great Depression. The country seemed to be coming apart when we needed desperately to be coming together.

I wanted to chart a new course rooted first in growth and opportunity—first, to put our economic house in order so that our businesses could prosper and create jobs; second, to tap the full potential of the new global economy; third, to invest in our people so that they would have the capacity to meet the demands of this new age and to improve their own lives.

This strategy is in place, and it is working. The deficit is half of what it was. The government is now the smallest it's been in thirty years. As a percentage of the federal work force, the federal government's the smallest it's been since 1933, before the beginning of the New Deal. We signed over two hundred trade agreements. Our exports are at an all-time high. Fifteen million of our hardest-pressed people have gotten tax cuts; most of small businesses have as well. We've invested in research and defense transformations. We've invested in new technologies. And we've invested in environmental protection and sustainable development.

And I will say parenthetically, the great challenge of your age will be to prove that we can bring prosperity and opportunity to people all across the globe without destroying the environment, which is the precondition of our successful existence. And all of you will have to meet that challenge, and I challenge you to do it.

Our economy, while most of the rest of the world was in

recession, has produced 8.5 million new jobs; the lowest combined rates of inflation, unemployment, and home mortgages in three decades; the lowest deficit as a percentage of our income of any advanced economy in the world; 3.7 million more American homeowners; and record numbers of new small businesses in each of the last three years. We are doing well, but we must do better if we are going to make the promise of this new age real to all Americans. That means we have to grow faster. How fast can we grow? No one knows the exact answer to that. But if we look at the long term, if we believe in our people and invest in them and their opportunities and our people take responsibility, the sky is the limit.

We must look with the greatest skepticism toward those who promise easy and quick solutions.

We know that the course, at least long-term growth, is in the minds and spirits and ideas and discipline and effort of people like those of you who graduate here today.

We are on the right course. We must accelerate it, not veer from it. We have to finish the job we started in 1993 and balance the budget, not only because we want to free you and your children of the legacy of debt, but because that will keep interest rates down, increase savings, expand companies, start new small businesses, help more families buy a home and more parents send their children to college.

We know we have to continue the fight for fair and open trade because we've proved now if other markets are as open to our products and services as we are to theirs, we'll do just fine.

We know we have to do more to help all Americans deal with the economic changes of the present day in a more positive way by investing in the future and targeting tax cuts to help Americans deal with their own problems and build strong families.

We know we have to continue to invest in the things that a government needs to invest in, including research and development and technology and environmental protection.

We know that since so many people will have to change jobs more often than in the past, we have to give families the security to know if they change jobs, they can still carry with them access to health care and pensions and education for a lifetime.

But finally, and most importantly, if we really want Americans, all Americans, to participate in the future that is now at your fingertips, we have got to increase the quality and the level of education, not just for the graduates of Princeton and Georgetown and Yale and the state universities of this country but for all the American people. It is the only way to achieve that goal.

The very fact that we have been here—or our forebears have—for 250 years is testimony to the elemental truth that education has always been important to individual Americans. And for quite a long time education has been quite important to our whole country. Fifty years ago, when the Class of '46 was here, coming in after World War II, the GI Bill helped to build a great American middle class and a great American economy. But today, more than ever before in the history of the United States, education is the fault line, the great continental divide between those who will prosper and those who will not in the new economy.

If you look at the census data, you can see what happens to hardworking people who have a high-school diploma or who drop out of high school and try to keep up in the job market but fall further and further behind. You can also see that if all Americans have access to education, it is no longer a fault line; it is a sturdy bridge that will lead us all together, from the old economy to the new.

Now, we have to work to give every American that kind

of opportunity. And we've worked hard to do it, from increasing preschool opportunities to improving the public school years, to increasing technology in our schools. This spring the Vice President and I helped to kick off a Net Day in California, where schools and businesses and civic leaders hooked up nearly 50 percent of the schools to the Internet in a single weekend. What I want to see is every schoolroom and every library and every school in America hooked up to the Internet by the year 2000. We can do that....

... Just consider the last hundred years. At the turn of the century the progressives made it the law of the land for every child to be in school. Before then there was no such requirement. After World War II, we said ten years are not enough, public schools should extend to twelve years. And then, as I said, the GI Bill and college loans threw open the doors of college to the sons and daughters of farmers and factory workers, and they have powered our economy ever since.

America knows that higher education is the key to the growth we need to lift our country, and today that is more true than ever. Just listen to these facts. Over half the new jobs created in the last three years have been managerial and professional jobs. The new jobs require a higher level of skills.

Fifteen years ago the typical worker with a college degree made 38 percent more than a worker with a high school diploma. Today that figure is 73 percent more. Two years of college means a 20 percent increase in annual earnings. People who finish two years of college earn a quarter of a million dollars more than their high school counterparts over a lifetime.

Now it is clear that America has the best higher education system in the world and that it is the key to a successful future in the twenty-first century. It is also clear that because of costs and other factors, not all Americans have access to higher education. I want to say today that I believe the clear facts of this time make it imperative that our goal must be nothing less than to make the thirteenth and fourteenth years of education as universal to all Americans as the first twelve are today.

I know that here at the Reunion Weekend the Class of '46 has celebrated its fiftieth reunion, and I want to just mention them one more time. Many members of the Class of '46 fought in the Second World War, and they came home and laid down their arms and took up the responsibility of the future with the help of the GI Bill. That's when our nation did its part simply by giving them the opportunity to make the most of their own lives. And in doing that, they made America's most golden years. The ultimate lesson of the Class of 1946 will also apply to the Class of 1996 in the twenty-first century. Because of the education you have, if America does well, you will do very well. If America is a good country to live in, you will be able to build a very good life.

So I ask you never to be satisfied with an age of probability for only the sons and daughters of Princeton. You could go your own way in a society that after all seems so often to be coming apart instead of coming together. You will of course have the ability to succeed in a global economy even if you have to secede from those Americans trapped in the old economy. But you should not walk away from our common purpose. Again, I will say this is about far more than economics and money. It is about preserving the quality of our democracy; the integrity of every person standing as an equal citizen before the law; the ability of our country to prove that no matter how diverse we get, we can still come together in shared community values to make each of our lives, and our families' lives, stronger and richer and better. This is about more than money.

The older I get and the more I become aware that I have

more yesterdays than tomorrows, the more I think that in our final hours, which all of us have to face, very rarely will we say, "Gosh, I wish I had spent more time at the office," or, "If only I had made just a little more money." But we will think about the dreams we lived out, the wonders we knew, when we were most fully alive.

This is about giving every single solitary soul in this country the chance to be most fully alive. And if we do that, those of you who have this brilliant education, who have been gifted by God with great minds and strong bodies and hearts—you will do very well, and you will be very happy.

In 1914 Woodrow Wilson wrote, as President: "The future is clear and bright with the promise of the best things. We are all in the same boat. We shall advance and advance together with a new spirit."

I wish you well. And I pray that you will advance and advance together with a new spirit. God bless you, and God bless America.

Ken Burns

Hampshire College
May 16, 1987

Ken Burns is best known as the director and creator of The
Civil War, *a sprawling, eleven-hour epic documentary of
America's most bloody conflict. When the film aired on PBS in
1990, it became the most popular program ever shown on
public television. After graduating from Hampshire College in
1975, he directed and produced* The Brooklyn Bridge *(1981),
receiving an Academy Award nomination for best documentary.
He later made* Huey Long *(1985),* The Statue of Liberty
(1985), and The Congress *(1989). Burns received Academy
Award and Emmy nominations for* The Statue of Liberty.
After the success of The Civil War, *Burns made the successful
nine-hour documentary* Baseball *in 1994.*

. . . Ladies and gentlemen, all the Hampshire community, I
am deeply honored to be here in this place for this wonderful
occasion.

It did, however, come to my attention that Roger Clemens
and Woody Allen were also under consideration to give this
address. Well, let me reassure you that I *happen* to possess
the fastball of Woody Allen and *certainly* the existential angst
of Roger Clemens. Needless to say, when I was asked to do
this, my first thought was: My God, who can I get to serve
on my committee?

No, my first thoughts ranged to my own graduation from
Hampshire twelve years ago. In a way I was born here at
Hampshire, and that final day, so much like today, remains

in my mind with a special clarity. Things were different: My hair was down to my waist; my feet were bare. My future wife sat in the audience, as she does today with our two daughters. John Boyle, now the late John Boyle, that marvelous, large, ruddy, Irish sheriff of Hampshire County, opened the ceremonies, as he has so many times, bellowing his wonderful "Gawd," and I am sure he would have spelled it G-A-W-D, "Gawd bless the commonwealth of Massachusetts." I remember sitting in the audience and realizing what a great word "commonwealth" was. For the first time it had real meaning. In that moment of openness the word went straight into my heart. It's still there, thankfully. Commonwealth.

As I look around, things feel different. There are more buildings, and Bob Stiles, whose land and life surround us, is gone. Twelve years ago it was a very different world, and in many ways Hampshire was a very different college. At that time we were not so sure what a diploma from Hampshire meant, whether we were going out into the world with live ammunition. Nineteen seventy-five was when the me generation was in full swing, the sixties' energy that had in part given birth to Hampshire abruptly ended. All of a sudden it seemed that nearly everyone else was graduating from college with this all-important mystical gift called income earning potential.

Back at Hampshire, we felt our investment with college was more personal, more honest, more involved, but frankly a lot was unknown. And very new.

Well, I am pleased to report to you how valued a Hampshire student is out there. It took a little time, but in a sense the coast is clear, and the gun *is* loaded. It is now "okay" to be from Hampshire. In fact you will find yourself welcome all over—in graduate schools, in business, in the artistic community. It is still called that hippie school, but the relative few who possess a Hampshire education are prized and proof of the extraordinary success of this experiment.

But with that success comes a tremendous responsibility that you now share. Those you leave behind here, as well as the subsequent classes that pass through, will of course have to struggle constantly to keep this an ongoing experiment, to keep the cement from hardening. But you now have to reflect the best of the Hampshire experience and put it into practice, make it come alive. You are now afflicted in a very real sense with the dreaded *non satis scire* disease.

There is no cure. *Non satis scire.* To know is not enough. What Hampshire is trying to say, and what you will find so extremely valuable when you get out, is that you can accumulate not just knowledge but how to use that knowledge, and then, when you are in life, you will have a creative relationship with the problems, the processes of the world. And that's what life is about. It's not knowing the answers; it's having a relationship with the problems. And you will find that Hampshire arms you in the best kind of way. You belong to a commonwealth.

Of course Hampshire is not perfect. No college is. You will find gaps, things missing that Hampshire didn't give. But we, you and I, have a wonderful advantage. We know where and how to look.

So many of the things we celebrate today, let us, like the Philippines celebrating democracy,* celebrate innovation and the tremendous energy that is released in it. You have felt it here, and with a true course you will continue to experience it and invest it with new meaning no matter what road you

---

*After twenty years of strict, repressive government under President Ferdinand Marcos, Corazón Aquino, the widow of murdered Marcos opponent Benigno Aquino, became president in 1987, bringing democracy to the island nation.

take. Good luck to you. It is also reassuring to know that fairly soon we won't have to talk about Hampshire so much. To others. To ourselves. The college is growing. We will be grown up, and that is truly something to celebrate.

When I began to prepare for this address, I spoke to a number of friends who (because of their distinguished work) had practice with this sort of thing. Their advice and collective wisdom was very helpful. One said to avoid clichés like the plague. Another gave the best advice for me (and for you): Be yourself. But one said, "By all means, don't tell them their future lies ahead of them. That's the worst."

I thought about this, and I think our future lies behind us. In our past, personal and collective. In the last dozen years I have learned many things, but that history is our greatest teacher is perhaps the most important lesson. I now feel like I am an American possession, like Samoa or Guam. I am possessed by American history.

However, this enthusiasm is by no means shared by all. History, and its valuable advice, continues to recede in importance in schools all over. The statistics are now frightening. A majority of high school seniors do not know who Joseph Stalin or Winston Churchill were. They did not know, of the Declaration of Independence, the Bill of Rights, and the Emancipation Proclamation, which came first. And a majority could not tell the correct half century in which the Civil War took place. The most important event of our past.

So I would like to talk briefly about history. About remembering and forgetting. About things that are coming up in our world that reverberate with our past.

We Americans tend to ignore our past. Perhaps we fear having one and burn it behind us like rocket fuel, always looking forward, refashioning history into a Madison Avenue–style hybrid with few blemishes. And that's a bad thing.

The consequences are not just ignorance or stupidity or even repeating. It represents the deepest kind of inattention, and it becomes a tear or a gap in who we are.

I think that in each of my own films, and with each film more strongly and completely, I have been seized or possessed by an aspect of American history, something that spoke of the aspirations and struggles and motives of people, in the Brooklyn Bridge, in the Statue of Liberty or the Shakers, something that went to the heart of who we have been, to become what we are. And I think that with each film, each story I have struggled with, my sense has sharpened that a thread runs through all the stories, connects these histories one to the other.

That thread is the essential American one: the struggle for human freedom, whether of movement and design, of sheer achievement in the Brooklyn Bridge, or of political freedom in the Statue of Liberty, or of spiritual freedom, freedom of the hand and heart, in the experience of the Shakers. And I know this is what has drawn me to the Civil War, for in that war the issue of human freedom came for this country, for our people, to the profoundest and most tragic crux. The historian Shelby Foote has called it the crossroads in our being, but somehow, when we crossed over, we forgot where we had been. I think of what James Symington, a former congressman and father of a Hampshire student, said in an interview for our film last year. Slavery, he said, was merely the horrible statutory expression of a deeper rift between peoples based on race, and this rift is what we struggle still to erase from the hearts and minds of people.

That rift stands at the very center of American history; it is the great challenge to which all our deepest aspirations to freedom must rise. If we forget that, if we forget the great stain of slavery that stands at the heart of our history, we forget who we are, and we make the rift deeper and wider, and that's what forgetting is: making the human rift wider.

And we are forgetting it even now, on campuses and in suburbs and cities, forgetting that after all, only 127 years ago 4 million Americans were owned by other Americans, that 630,000 Americans died over the issue, when our population was a mere 30 million. Two percent died.

We too often tend to think, and this is part of the forgetting, that those people, those Americans, were not the same as us, and thus we cut the thread of identity and responsibility that really binds us to them all the same. But they were very like us. They were health faddists and faith healers, into nature cures, water cures, free love, and women's rights; there was evangelical fervor, spiritual experiment, and religious movements of every kind. But they were (sharply) worldly realists too. Two days after the First Battle of Bull Run in July of 1861, canny real estate speculators bought up the battlefield to make a second kind of killing as a tourist site.

Our affinity with them comes in a blizzard of facts. There were 450 brothels in Washington, D.C., alone during the Civil War; the Union men called a trip to one "going down the line" and spoke of taking "horizontal refreshment." Men like Jay Gould and J. P. Morgan bought inside government knowledge of military situations, then used it to make millions. Philip Armour gave up gold mining to strike it rich packing pork for the Union Army and, what is worse, thereby inventing Spam.

I recently read something that struck me very deeply. "From whence shall we expect the approach of danger?" the writer asked. "Shall some trans-Atlantic giant step the earth and crush us at a blow? Never. All the armies of Europe and Asia could not by force take a drink from the Ohio River or make a track on the Blue Ridge in the trial of a thousand years. If destruction be our lot we must ourselves be its authors and finishers. As a nation of free men we will live forever or die by suicide."

This could have been written today. It was written 140 years ago, well before the Civil War, by Abraham Lincoln, who presided over the nearest attempt at national suicide Americans ever made. And *they* killed each other over the meaning of freedom in America. We should remember that.

But the forgetting begins early and continues. Photography came of an age with the Civil War, and more than a million images were taken in four years for a public obsessed with seeing, and perhaps also thereby subduing, the shock and carnage they were inflicting on one another. But the public appetite for war photographs, fantastic during the war, dropped off sharply after Appomattox. Mathew Brady went bankrupt. Thousands of photographs were lost, forgotten, mislaid, or misused. Glass plate negatives were often sold to gardeners, not for their images but for the glass itself. In the years immediately following Appomattox, the sun slowly burned the filmy image of war from countless greenhouse gardens across the country, as if the memories might be erased. Still later the glass would be used as lenses in the faceplates of World War I gas masks.

So it comes *down* to us, whether we know it, or want to know it, or not. I think we must want to know it, and to know it, we must listen to it and see it, not let the image fade. It is alarming to reflect upon how many of the burning issues that for some reason seemed self-evident twenty years ago have faded from public concern in the last twelve, since I graduated here with my bare feet and my hair down my back. It is not enough to blame it all on the ultimate glass plate negative, TV. We must take more responsibility for our memories than that.

A few weeks ago I was in New Orleans and saw an old

friend, a retired judge named Cecil Morgan. Cecil was a fierce opponent of Huey Long's in the Louisiana legislature in the thirties, but that's another story. This time he brought out for me an old book written by his ancestor, James Morris Morgan, who had fought with the Confederates in the Civil War. It was called *Recollections of a Rebel Reefer*—a reference to a midshipman in the Navy, by the way. But what really caught my eye was a letter stuck in the book, a letter to old James Morgan's great-niece Louise. Let me read it to you:

Dear Louise,

When the incidents recorded in this volume seem ancient to you, try to realize that I can remember your grandfather's grandmother Morgan and her tales of how she danced with George Washington.

The past to the aged does not seem as far away as does the dim future, and the only thing that abides with us always is the love of those who are dear to us.

Affectionately, your old great-uncle,
James Morris Morgan

What I am trying to say in all of this is that there is a profound connection between remembering and freedom and human attachment. That's what history is to me. And forgetting is the opposite of all that: It is a kind of slavery and the worst kind of human detachment. Somewhere in the Statue of Liberty film, a film I made with another Hampshire graduate, Buddy Squiers, the writer James Baldwin remarked that no one was ever born who agreed to be a slave. But then, he continued, multitudes and multitudes of people enslave *themselves* every hour of every day to this or that doctrine, this or that delusion of safety, this or that lie:

Anti-Semites are slaves to delusion; people who hate Negroes are slaves; people who love money are slaves. We are living in a universe really of willing slaves, Baldwin said, which is what makes the concept of liberty and the concept of freedom so dangerous.

And which is why we must remember, even when, precisely when, what memory has to tell us is appalling. It has seemed to me that the meaning of our freedom as Americans is the freedom of memory, which is also a kind of obligation. We must remember that our country was born under the sign that all men were created equal, but we must remember also that that proclamation did not include blacks or women or the poor. We must remember that Abraham Lincoln signed the Emancipation Proclamation, but we must also remember that Lincoln thought of recolonizing black Americans to Panama or Africa as late as April of 1861 as the guns opened up at Fort Sumter. We must remember that the Thirteenth and Fourteenth Amendments secured some kind of equality before the law for blacks. But we must also remember that equality as a human fact did not come at once, has still to come, and if we do not believe that, *we forget.*

So what do we make of all this? Let me speak directly to the graduating class. As you pursue the future, your future, pursue the past. Let it be your guide. Know the history of your country, not because it is knowledge to accumulate but because it arms you in the best kind of way.

Learn about your family. Find out about your grandmother's grandfather. Where was he in 1861? It will help you, I promise. Read about your history. Read David McCullough's *The Great Bridge*, the best love story around. Read about Sam Houston and his remarkable life. Find out about the real Martin Luther King, not the instant image of him but the student of Gandhi. Read Shelby Foote's stunning history of the Civil War; he is the closest thing we have to Homer.

Read Mary Chesnut's Diary, the best diary kept during that period.

Stay involved with the college as you move on. Hampshire, to thrive, will need your attention and your tinkering. And cherish your teachers. I have spoken a little today of memory, attachment, freedom. Let me freely acknowledge my attachments. A very large one is to this college, my birthplace, but I count as one of the great pleasures of my life my association with Jerry Liebling. (What you see in my work that you like is Jerry. Everything else is just Ken.)

There is a cartoon I saw recently which pictures a group of men standing in hell, the flames licking up around them. One man is speaking to the others; he says, "Apparently over two hundred screen credits didn't mean a damn thing." Avoid the word "career" and even "profession." They are concerned with money and position. Continue to investigate.

Have a style, by all means have a style, but remember that fashion itself has a cold center. There is nothing behind it.

Travel. Don't get stuck in one place. I was fortunate this year to see four different springs. In Louisiana, Missouri, Virginia, and now New England. This is your annual chance to learn about the thousand shades of green there are. It is a tonic.

Whatever you do, walk over the Brooklyn Bridge.

You might even visit Appomattox, where the country was reunited. Finally, Shelby Foote once wrote, "This new unity was best defined, perhaps, by the change in number of a simple verb. In common speech, abroad as well as on this side of the ocean, once the nation emerged from the crucible of that war, 'the United States *are*' became 'the United States *is*.' "

Do not neglect your work, but start families. Make babies, lots of them. Say twenty-five. Send them all to Hampshire.

God bless the commonwealth of Massachusetts.

Madeleine Albright

Mount Holyoke College
May 25, 1997

*In 1997 Madeleine K. Albright became the first female
secretary of state in U.S. history, and she is currently the
highest-ranking woman in the U.S. government. Previously
Albright served as the U.S. permanent representative to the
United Nations, president of the Center for National Policy,
and director of the Women in Foreign Service program at
Georgetown University's prestigious School of Foreign Service.
In this address to the all-female graduating class of Mount
Holyoke, Albright discusses the state of America and the world
and the place for women in the new century.*

To the entire Mount Holyoke community, I say thank you
for the invitation to be here and thank you very much for
the honorary degree.

To the parents of the Class of '97, I know how you feel.
I have had three daughters graduate from college, and always
the emotions are mixed. You feel one part sad, one part
relieved, one part broke, and every part proud.

To the graduates, I offer my heartfelt congratulations. This
is the payoff for all the late nights in the library and the long
hours studying. In the years ahead you will look back upon
this ceremony and realize that today—May 25, 1997—was
the very day you began to forget everything you learned in
college.

You will find slipping from your mind the carefully memorized names of eighteenth-century composers, European monarchs, and the various body parts of dissected frogs. But as your hopes for hitting the jackpot on *Jeopardy!* fade, you will find the more profound aspects of a Mount Holyoke education endure.

According to the brochure, "Mount Holyoke is a universe where the life of the mind is intensely lived, a space apart where women may imagine themselves and go forward— pioneers still—to transform the world."

To the extent that description is true—and I can see from your faces that it is—you will be thankful all your lives.

In school, grades and test results measure accomplishment. You know what is expected and where you stand.

But once you leave school, you will have to rely upon an inner compass. Whether you are an aspiring scientist or CEO, poet or President—or all of the above—each day you will face decisions that test your courage, values, and sense of self. To this dilemma there is no sure remedy. Not even Rosie O'Donnell can draw for you a road map to a life of fulfillment and accomplishment.

But Mount Holyoke has given you the tools you need to draw your own.

This year you celebrate at this storied college the bicentennial of Mary Lyon, your founder, who almost single-handedly brought women's education into the nineteenth-century from where it had previously been—which is roughly the twelfth.

Your campus here is beautiful, your reputation is the best, your leadership is strong, and each of your students is brilliant, creative, open-minded, and blessed with good posture.

If ever an institution might be tempted by complacency, yours is it.

Instead, through "Mount Holyoke 2003," you are drafting a blueprint for the future. You are debating—rather vigorously, I understand—the proper direction for your college, recognizing that excellence is never a state of being, but always of becoming.

Your individual choices and challenges, and those of this college, have their parallel in options now facing the United States.

America has arrived at the threshold of a new century strong, respected, prosperous, and with no single powerful enemy against whom we must lock our gates.

Hitler is dead. Stalin is dead. Lenin is dead. And the only Marx that still matters is on late-night television shooting elephants in their pajamas.

The temptation is to coast. To sit back, avert our eyes, and assume that what does not affect us immediately will not affect us ever.

But then we have to ask: What if, half a century ago, Secretary of State George Marshall had decided that America had done enough in helping to win the Second World War and that we could let a Europe in ruins fend for itself?

What if President Truman had decided that the surrounded city of Berlin was too remote and that Americans were too weary of conflict and too wary of new commitments to mount an airlift on its behalf?

What if Eleanor Roosevelt had decided that it was enough for Americans to worry about the rights of our own citizens and that we did not need to lead in forging the Universal Declaration of Human Rights?

As individuals each of us must choose whether to live our lives narrowly, selfishly, and complacently or to act with courage and faith.

As a nation America must choose whether to turn inward and betray the lessons of history or to seize the opportunity before us to shape history. Today, under the leadership of President Clinton, America is making the right choice.

The Berlin Wall is now a memory. We could be satisfied with that. Instead we are enlarging and adapting NATO and striving to create a future for Europe in which every democracy—including Russia—is our partner and every partner is a builder of peace.

Largely because of U.S. leadership, nuclear weapons no longer target our homes. We could relax. Instead we are working to reduce nuclear arsenals further, eliminate chemical weapons, end the child-maiming scourge of land mines, and ratify a treaty that would ban nuclear explosions forever.

The fighting in Bosnia has stopped. We could turn our backs now and risk renewed war. Instead we are renewing our commitment and insisting that the parties meet theirs, to implement the Dayton Accords. And we are backing the War Crimes Tribunal, because we believe that those responsible for ethnic cleansing should be held accountable and those who consider rape just another tactic of war should answer for their crimes.

We have built a growing world economy in which those with modern skills and available capital have done very well. We could stop there. Instead we are pursuing a broader prosperity, in which those entrapped by poverty and discrimination are empowered to share and in which every democracy on every continent will be included.

In our lifetimes we have seen enormous advances in the status of women. We could now lower our voices and—as some suggest—sit sedately down. Instead women everywhere—whether bumping against a glass ceiling or rising from a dirt floor—are standing up, spreading the word that we are ready to claim our rightful place as full citizens and full participants in every society on earth.

Mount Holyoke is the home, to borrow Wendy Wasserstein's phrase, of "uncommon women." But we know that there are uncommon women in all corners of the globe.

In recent years I have met in Sarajevo with women weighted down by personal grief reaching out across ethnic lines to rebuild their shattered society.

In Burundi I have seen women taking the lead in efforts to avoid the fate of neighboring Rwanda, where violence left three quarters of the population female, and one half of the women widows.

In Guatemala I have talked to women striving to ensure that their new peace endures and is accompanied by justice and an end to discrimination and abuse.

And in Burma I have met with a remarkable woman named Aung San Suu Kyi, who risks her life every day to keep alive the hope for democracy in her country.

These women have in common a determination to chart their own path and, by so doing, to alter for the better the course of their country or community.

Each has suffered blows, but each has proceeded with courage. Each has persevered.

As you go along your own road in life, you will, if you aim high enough, also meet resistance, for as Robert Kennedy once said, "If there's nobody in your way, it's because you're not going anywhere." But no matter how tough the opposition may seem, have courage still—and persevere.

There is no doubt, if you aim high enough, that you will be confronted by those who say that your efforts to change the world or improve the lot of those around you do not mean much in the grand scheme of things. But no matter how impotent you may sometimes feel, have courage still—and persevere.

It is certain, if you aim high enough, that you will find your strongest beliefs ridiculed and challenged; principles that you cherish may be derisively dismissed by those claiming to be more practical or realistic than you. But no matter how weary you may become in persuading others to see the value in what you value, have courage still—and persevere.

Inevitably, if you aim high enough, you will be buffeted by demands of family, friends, and employment that will conspire to distract you from your course. But no matter how difficult it may be to meet the commitments you have made, have courage still—and persevere.

It has been said that all work that is worth anything is done in faith.

This morning, in these beautiful surroundings, at this celebration of warm memory and high expectation, I summon you in the name of this historic college and of all who have passed through its halls, to embrace the faith that your courage and your perseverance will make a difference and that every life enriched by your giving, every friend touched by your affection, every soul inspired by your passion, and every barrier to justice brought down by your determination will ennoble your own life, inspire others, serve your country, and explode outward the boundaries of what is achievable on this earth.

So congratulations, good luck, and remember always to sit up straight.

Thank you very much.

Tom Brokaw

Connecticut College
May 25, 1996

Tom Brokaw is the managing editor and anchor of the NBC
Evening News with Tom Brokaw. *He joined NBC News
in 1966 and became sole anchor of the* Evening News *in
1983. Among his many career highlights are groundbreaking
interviews with Mikhail Gorbachev and the Dalai Lama and
his reports from the Berlin Wall the night it fell. He is a two-
time Emmy Award winner.*

These are moments to be cherished in American life: The
realization of a common dream, unique, really to this land—a
college education, a privilege not confined to the wellborn or
wealthy. Here the working class sits side by side with old
and new fortunes; here new Americans from distant lands and
cultures mingle with the sons and daughters of the Americans
who came on sailing ships, some to proclaim their freedom,
others in the holds and chains of slave ships.

I am honored to be with you. I know what is expected of
me. Brevity, most of all. Maybe a little humor. Wisdom, or
the appearance of it. I am here as a journalist, but I am also
here as a husband, a father, and a citizen. That is the four-
part harmony of my life, and they are complementary parts;
I am incomplete if any one is missing.

I am also a child of the second half of the twentieth century. I was born in 1940, and my earliest memories are of the
pain and the glories of World War II; I came of an age with
the threat of nuclear war in the world and great inno-

cence at home; I stood on front lines of the battle for civil rights and am haunted still by the personal and political price this nation paid in Vietnam; I can tell you when I first heard Elvis and when I first saw the Beatles. One President was assassinated; another was forced to resign. Communism fell. Women in America began to take their rightful place. The American family began to take on new forms, alas, too often to the detriment of family members and society.

It was a time of momentous change. And it was merely an overture for your generation. The sound you hear is a new century, coming fast, with changes and challenges yet unimagined.

This is your time: the twenty-first century. The millennium. It is yours to shape and master. It makes my heart race. I envy you.

You have at your disposal a dazzling assortment of new tools not even imagined not so long ago. The gee whiz tools of communications and information: cable television, satellites, cell phones, pagers, faxes, and, of course, the king of them all, the personal computer. Who could ask for anything more?

Well, here is a modest suggestion as you lead us into the new century. This will be the cyberspace equivalent of a teenage joyride—reckless and pointless—unless we all apply the lessons of earlier technological revolutions to this one. They almost all have had unexpected consequences, and they are most successful when as much effort and thought is applied to the use of the technology as to the development of it in the first place.

If this new technology becomes simply another means of amusing ourselves or speeding the transactions of commerce or communicating simply for the sake of communication, then we will have failed.

If this new technology becomes primarily the province of

the privileged, leaving the underclass to wander in cyber-wilderness, then we will have failed.

This is your technology. Indeed with the introduction of the cyber age we have fundamentally altered a relationship between generations. This is the first time the kids have taught their parents to drive.

It's where we're headed that concerns me. One of my principal passions is the environment and biological diversity. Cybertechnology is a great vehicle for information exchange, mapping, and research. But if we become a nation of shut-ins, more engrossed in a virtual rain forest than the real, thick, seamy, green, vibrant, living, breathing experience, we will be poorer for it.

For all of its capacity, this new technology also is of little use in solving what I believe is the most vexing issue of American life: race. There is no delete button for bigotry. We may be color-blind as we surf the Net, but alas, on the street, in the workplace, in our homes and social life, we—more than we care to acknowledge—see life through a prism of pigmentation.

We're doing better. I grew up in apartheid America. Now we have the laws of the land, the richest tapestry of ethnic achievement and prominence, people of courage on all sides of the racial dynamic.

We are increasingly a land of many colors, a geography of Asian, Latino, and African hues against a diminishing back-drop of white European stock.

If we allow racism, expressed either as utter bigotry or dressed up as excessive ethnic pride, to metastasize at the current rates, we'll soon find ourselves at an incurable stage, unable to build walls high enough, schools private enough, industries insulated enough to withstand the ravages of racism.

It requires instead that most basic and most vexing human

condition: an open mind and an open heart. That can be your legacy.

We seem at the moment to be caught in a cycle of easy and cheap distractions. Celebrity has been at once devalued and raised to an artificially high place in our popular culture. Never mind achievement or worth that stands the test of time. A moment in the spotlight of television is life itself for dysfunctional families willing to share their sordid secrets on daytime talk shows, for parents to put their youngsters in the cockpits of small planes on stormy days,* for performers to reach ever further into the universe of the outrageous to make an impression, for producers and editors to succumb to the easy temptations of titillation rather than intellectual provocation.

And we encourage that by our benign attention.

Is that how we want to measure, in the closing days of the twentieth century, what has been called the American Century?

We're better than that, or we should be.

I've watched this country go from the vanilla fifties, to the psychedelic sixties, to the disco seventies, to the greedy eighties.

Now, in the uncertain nineties, what worries me most is the enduring cynicism in our land about the separation from the traditional institutions of public life, city hall, statehouse, especially Washington. I cannot remember a time when there was such recognition that the traditional framework of society—of family and faith and community and responsibility and accountability—was in such desperate need of repair.

Your immediate concerns, understandably, are jobs and ca-

---

*In April 1996, seven-year-old Jessica Dubroff and her father, Lloyd, were killed in a plane crash near Cheyenne, Wyoming. Jessica was piloting the plane in an attempt to become the youngest person to fly across the United States.

reers and relationships. Indeed. They will remain your primary focus, for they are about the personal happiness and survival.

However, the means by which your time will be measured will be the values that you embrace, the care that you show for each other. Yours can be the age of tolerance and understanding.

To be true to the meaning of this institution and the purpose of its education I urge you to remember the counsel of the late Bartlett Giamatti, Yale president, major league baseball commissioner, and Renaissance man. In a setting quite like this in a lesser-known eastern institution he said, "You must know that idealism is not a paralyzing but a liberating force and that to strive for principles, even if the journey is never completed, is to tap a vast source of energy, the energy to commit to your best in the brief, precious time that each of us is blessed to have."

Fifty years ago—in 1946—another generation of young Americans marked a special spring in their lives. Together with the British, other Western allies, and especially the Russians they had just won the war against Hitler and Nazi Germany and imperialist Japan. They had saved the world.

They came home, and they built the America we know today. They kept the peace. They went to college in historic proportions; they married and had families. They built giant industries and small businesses. They gave us great universities and great highway systems. They integrated America. They discovered new cures and gave us new songs. They rebuilt their enemies and stood tall against the new adversaries in Moscow and Beijing.

And they didn't whine or whimper.

I am in awe of them.

Fifty years from now let another commencement speaker

stand here and say of your generation, "They saved their world, and I am in awe of them."

This is your time. Take it on. Don't be afraid to lean into the wind, love the earth in all of its natural glories, and take care of each other. We're counting on you.

Ronald Reagan

University of Notre Dame
May 17, 1981

Ronald Reagan, the fortieth President of the United States, entered the White House in 1981 on a conservative platform that promised to reduce the size of the government, rebuild America's military might, and return America to more traditional values. The first actor ever to sit in the Oval Office, Reagan was best known for his role as George Gipp, the Notre Dame football star who died of pneumonia in the movie Knute Rockne—All American. *Reagan here uses the story of George Gipp to explain how self-sacrifice and doing things for others have made America great.*

. . . Nancy and I are greatly honored to share this day with you, and our pleasure has been more than doubled because I am also sharing the platform with a longtime dear friend, Pat O'Brien.

Pat and I haven't been able to see much of each other lately, so I haven't had a chance to tell him that there is now another tie that binds us together. Until a few weeks ago I knew very little about my father's ancestry. He had been orphaned at age six. But now I've learned that his grandfather, my great-grandfather, left Ireland to come to America, leaving his home in Ballyporeen, a village in County Tipperary in Ireland, and I have learned that Ballyporeen is the ancestral home of the O'Briens.

Now, if I don't watch out, this may turn out to be less of a commencement than a warm bath in nostalgic memories.

Growing up in Illinois, I was influenced by a sports legend so national in scope it was almost mystical. It is difficult to explain to anyone who didn't live in those times. The legend was based on a combination of three elements: a game, football; a university, Notre Dame; and a man, Knute Rockne. There has been nothing like it before or since.

My first time to ever see Notre Dame was to come here as a sports announcer, two years out of college, to broadcast a football game. You won or I wouldn't have mentioned it.

A number of years later I returned in the company of Pat O'Brien and a galaxy of Hollywood stars for the world premiere of *Knute Rockne—All American* in which I was privileged to play George Gipp. I've always suspected that there might have been many actors in Hollywood who could have played the part better, but no one could have wanted to play it more than I did. And I was given the part largely because the star of that picture, Pat O'Brien, kindly and generously held out a helping hand to a beginning young actor.

Having come from the world of sports, I'd been trying to write a story about Knute Rockne. I must confess that I had someone in mind to play the Gipper. On one of my sports broadcasts before going to Hollywood, I had told the story of his career and tragic death. I didn't have very many words on paper when I learned that the studio that employed me was already preparing a story treatment for that film. And that brings me to the theme of my remarks.

I'm the fifth President of the United States to address a Notre Dame commencement.* The temptation is great to use this forum as an address on a great international or national issue that has nothing to do with this occasion. Indeed this is somewhat traditional. So I wasn't surprised when I read in

---

*Franklin Delano Roosevelt, Dwight D. Eisenhower, Gerald Ford, and Jimmy Carter also have addressed Notre Dame graduates.

several reputable journals that I was going to deliver an address on foreign policy or on the economy. I'm not going to talk about either.

But by the same token, I'll try not to belabor you with some of the standard rhetoric that is beloved of graduation speakers. For example, I'm not going to tell you that "You know more today than you've ever known before or that you will ever know again." The other standby is, "When I was fourteen, I didn't think my father knew anything. By the time I was twenty-one, I was amazed how much the old gentleman had learned in seven years." And then, of course, the traditional and the standby is that "A university like this is a storehouse of knowledge because the freshmen bring in so much and the seniors take so little away."

You members of the graduating class of 18—or 1981—I don't really go back that far—are what behaviorists call achievers. And while you will look back with warm pleasure on your memories of these years that brought you here to where you are today, you are also, I know, looking at the future that seems uncertain to most of you but which, let me assure you, offers great expectations.

Take pride in this day. Thank your parents, as one on your behalf has already done here. Thank those who've been of help to you over the last four years. And do a little celebrating; you're entitled. This is your day, and whatever I say should take cognizance of that fact. It is a milestone in life, and it marks a time of change.

Winston Churchill during the darkest period of the Battle of Britain in World War II said: "When great causes are on the move in the world . . . we learn we are spirits, not animals, and that something is going on in space and time, and beyond space and time, which, whether we like it or not, spells duty."

Now, I'm going to mention again that movie that Pat and

I and Notre Dame were in because it says something about America. First, Knute Rockne as a boy came to America with his parents from Norway. And in the few years it took him to grow up to college age, he became so American that here at Notre Dame, he became an all-American in a game that is still, to this day, uniquely American.

As a coach he did more than teach young men how to play a game. He believed truly that the noblest work of man was building the character of man. And maybe that's why he was a living legend. No man connected with football has ever achieved the stature or occupied the singular niche in the nation that he carved out for himself, not just in a sport, but in our entire social structure.

Now, today I hear very often, "Win one for the Gipper," spoken in a humorous vein. Lately, I've been hearing it by congressmen who are supportive of the programs that I've introduced. But let's look at the significance of that story. Rockne could have used Gipp's dying words to win a game at any time. But eight years went by following the death of George Gipp before Rock revealed those dying words, his deathbed wish.

And then he told that story at halftime to a team that was losing and one of the only teams he had ever coached that was torn by dissension and jealousy and factionalism. The seniors on that team were about to close out their football careers without learning or experiencing any of the real values that the game had come to impart. None of them had known George Gipp. They were children when he played for Notre Dame. It was to this team that Rockne told the story and so inspired them that they rose above their personal animosities. For someone they had never known, they joined together in a common cause and attained the unattainable.

We were told when we were making the picture of one line that was spoken by a player during that game. We were actually afraid to put it in the picture. The man who carried the ball over for the winning touchdown was injured on the play. We were told that as he was lifted on the stretcher and carried off the field, he was heard to say, "That's the last one I can get for you, Gipper."

Now it's only a game. And maybe to hear it now, afterward—and this is what we feared—it might sound maudlin and not the way it was intended. But is there anything wrong with young people having an experience, feeling something so deeply, thinking of someone else to the point that they can give so completely of themselves? There will come times in the lives of all of us when we'll be faced with causes bigger than ourselves, and they won't be on a playing field.

This nation was born when a band of men, the Founding Fathers, a group so unique we've never seen their like since, rose to such selfless heights. Lawyers, tradesmen, merchants, farmers—fifty-six men achieved security and standing in life but valued freedom more. They pledged their lives, their fortunes, and their sacred honor. Sixteen of them gave their lives. Most gave their fortunes. All gave their sacred honor.

They gave us more than a nation. They brought to all mankind for the first time the concept that man was born free, that each of us has inalienable rights, ours by the grace of God, and that government was created by us for our convenience, having only the powers that we choose to give it. This is the heritage that you're about to claim as you come out and join the society made up of those who have preceded you by a few years, or some of us by a great many.

The experiment of man's relation to man is a few years into its third century. Saying that may make it sound quite old. But let's look at it from another viewpoint or perspective. A few years ago someone figured out that if you could condense the entire history of life on earth into a motion picture that would run for twenty-four hours a day, 365 days a year—maybe on leap years we could have an intermission—this idea that is the United States wouldn't appear on the screen until three and a half seconds before midnight on December 31. And in those three and one-half seconds not only would a new concept of society come into being, a golden hope for all mankind, but more than half the activity, economic activity in world history, would take place on this continent. Free to express their genius, Americans, men and women, in three and one-half seconds, would perform such miracles of invention, construction, and production as the world had never seen. . . .

. . . I hope that when you leave this campus that you will do so with a feeling of obligation to your alma mater. She will need your help and support in the years to come. If ever the great independent colleges and universities like Notre Dame give way and are replaced by tax-supported institutions, the struggle to preserve academic freedom will have been lost.

We're troubled today by economic stagnation, brought on by inflated currency and prohibitive taxes and burdensome regulations. The cost of stagnation in human terms, mostly among those least equipped to survive it, is cruel and inhuman.

Now, after those remarks, don't decide that you better turn your diploma back in so you can stay another year on the campus. I've just given you the bad news. The good news is that something is being done about all this because the people of America have said, "Enough already." You know, we who had preceded you had just gotten so busy that we let things get out of hand. We forgot that we were the keepers of the power, forgot to challenge the notion that the state is the principal vehicle of social change, forgot that millions of social interactions among free individuals and institutions can do more to foster economic social progress than all the careful schemes of government planners.

Well, at last we're remembering, remembering that government has certain legitimate functions, which it can perform very well, that it can be responsive to the people, that it can be humane and compassionate, but that when it undertakes tasks that are not its proper province, it can do none of them as well or as economically as the private sector.

For too long government has been fixing things that aren't broken and inventing miracle cures for unknown diseases.

We need you. We need your youth. We need your strength. We need your idealism to help us make right that which is wrong. Now, I know that this period in your life you have been and are critically looking at the mores and customs of the past and questioning their value. Every generation does that. May I suggest, don't discard the time-tested values upon which civilization was built just because they're old. More important, don't let today's doom criers and cynics persuade you that the best is past and that from here on it's all downhill. Each generation sees farther than the generation that preceded it because it stands on the shoulders of that generation. You're going to have opportunities beyond anything that we've ever known. . . .

Susan Sontag

Wellesley College
June 3, 1983

Susan Sontag first gained national attention when the Partisan
Review *published her article "Notes on 'Camp' " in 1964. A
commentator on the mores of America, Sontag has written*
Against Interpretation, Styles of Radical Will, Under the
Sign of Saturn, Illness as Metaphor, *and* The Volcano
Lover. *In this speech at Wellesley College, Sontag urges
graduates to practice the age-old art of being stubborn.*

Graduation is one of the few genuine rites of passage left in
our society. You are, individually and collectively, passing
symbolically from one place to another, from an old to a new
status. And like all such rites, it is both retrospective and
prospective. You are graduating (or being graduated) from
college, which is the end of something. But the ceremony we
are participating in is called commencement.

That necessarily seasonal, minor literary form called the
commencement address also faces two directions. It usually
starts with an analysis of the society or the era—appropriately
pessimistic. It generally concludes with a grand exhortation,
in which the young graduates are urged to be, nonetheless,
of good cheer as they go forth into the arena of struggle that
is your life and this world.

As a writer, therefore fascinated by genres, as well as an
American and therefore prone to sermonizing, I shall respect
the tradition. The times we live in are indeed alarming. It is
a time of the most appalling escalation of violence—violence

to the environment, both "nature" and "culture"; violence to all living beings. A time in which the technology of exterminism, institutionalized in the nuclear arms race, has gained increasing credence—threatening life itself. It is also a time of a vertiginous drop in cultural standards, of virulent anti-intellectualism, and of triumphant mediocrity—a mediocrity that characterizes the educational system that you have just passed through, or has passed you through (for all the efforts and goodwill of many of your teachers). Trivializing standards, using as their justification the ideal of democracy, have made the very idea of a serious humanist education virtually unintelligible to most people. A vast system of mental lobotomization has been put into operation that sets the standards to which all accede. (I am speaking of course, of American television.) A singularly foolish and incompetent President sets the tone for an extraordinary regression in public ideals, strengthening apathy and a sense of hopelessness before the self-destructive course of foreign policy and the arms race. The best critical impulses in our society—such as that which has given rise to feminist consciousness—are under vicious attack. An increasing propaganda for conformism in morals and in art instructs us that originality and individuality will always be defeated and simply do not pay.

Of course the grim assessments of our era—such as I have just outlined—can themselves become a species of conformity. But only if we have too simple a sense of our lives. Whenever we speak, we tend to make matters sound simpler than they are and than we know they are.

I have said that this rite of passage—commencement—is one that faces in two directions. Your old status and your new status. The past and the present. The present and the future. But perhaps that is not just a description of today's exercises but a model for how you should try to live. As if you were always graduating, ending, and, simultaneously, always beginning. And your sense of the world, and of the large amount of life before you, also should face in two directions. It is true that the macronews—the news about the world—is bad. It is also true that your news may not be bad, indeed that you have a duty not to let it be as bad for you. Perhaps the main point of knowing a rule is to be an exception to it.

If your liberal arts education has meant anything, it has given you some notions of a critical opposition to the way things are. (And are generally defined—for example, for you as women.) This attitude of opposition is not justified as strategy, as a means to an end: a way of changing the world. It is, rather, the best way of being in the world.

As individuals we are never outside of some system which bestows significance. But we can become aware that our lives consist, both really and potentially, of many systems. That we always have choices, options—and that it is a failure of imagination (or fantasy) not to perceive this. The large system of significance in which we live is called culture. In that sense no one is without a culture. But in a stricter sense culture is not a given but an achievement that we have to work at all our lives. Far from being given, culture is something we have to strive to protect against all incursions. Culture is the opposite of provinciality—the provinciality of the intellect, the provinciality of the heart. (Far from being merely national, or local, it is properly international.) The highest culture is self-critical and makes us suspicious and critical of state power.

The liberal arts education you have received is not a luxury, as some of you may think, but a necessity—and more. For there is an intrinsic connection between a liberal arts education, by which I mean an education in the traditions and methods of "high" culture, and the very existence of liberty. Liberty means the right to diversity, to difference; the right to difficulty. It is the study of history and philosophy—it is the love of the arts, in all the nonlinear complexity of their traditions—that teaches us that.

Perhaps the most useful suggestion I can make, on the day when most of you are ceasing to be students, is that you go on being students for the rest of your lives. Don't move to a mental slum.

If you go on being students, if you do not consider you have graduated and that your schooling is done, perhaps you can at least save yourselves. And thereby make a space for others, in which they too can resist the pressures to conformity, the public drone. And the inner and outer censors, such as those who can tell you that you belong to a "postfeminist generation."

There are other counsels that might be useful. But if I had to restrict myself to just one, I would want to praise the virtue of obstinacy. (This is something anyone who is a writer knows a good deal about, for without obstinacy, or stubbornness, or tenacity, or pigheadedness, nothing gets written.) For whatever you want to do, if it has any quality or distinction or creativity—or, as women, if it defies sexual stereotypes—you can be sure that most people and many institutions will be devoted to encouraging you not to do it. If you want to do creative work—if you want, even though women, to lead unservile lives—there will be many obstacles. And you will have many excuses. These do not mitigate the failure. "Whatever prevents you from doing your work," a writer once observed, "has become your work."

All counsels of courage usually contain at the end a counsel of prudence. In Spenser's *Fairie Queene*, Book III, there is a place called the Castle of Busirane, on whose outer gate is written "BE BOLD," and on the second gate, "BE BOLD, BE BOLD," and on the inner iron door, "BE NOT TOO BOLD." This is not the advice I am giving. I would urge you to be as impudent as you dare. BE BOLD, BE BOLD, BE BOLD. Keep on reading. (Poetry. And novels from 1700 to 1940.) Lay off the television. And remember, when you hear yourself saying one day that you don't have the time anymore to read—or listen to music, or look at painting, or go to the movies, or do whatever feeds your head now—then you're getting old. That means they got you after all.

I wish you love. Courage. And fantasy.

Federico Peña

University of Texas
May 24, 1994

*Federico Peña has had a distinguished career in public
service. In 1992 President Clinton appointed him secretary
of transportation, making him the first Hispanic American ever
to hold a Cabinet position. A graduate of the University of
Texas, Peña returned with his parents in 1994, to deliver this
impassioned call to graduates.*

It is a great honor and a great joy for me to come home to
UT. To all who graduate today I have just one word to say:
congratulations! Your mothers and fathers and grandparents
and uncles and aunts and sisters and friends are proud of you,
and for good reason. This is your day.

You've passed the last final, your thesis has been accepted,
and thank God, your name was on the list for a cap and
gown. Tonight you take with you not just the knowledge
you gained but the friends you've made and the values you've
acquired. Best of all, and I'm living proof, you can come
back again. And when you do, UT will still feel like home.

For me, coming back brings back the late 1960s, when I
was here. The Longhorns fielded great teams; the Beatles had
a great new album, *Sergeant Pepper's Lonely Hearts Club Band.*
... Please tell me you remember the Beatles! And Mickey
Mouse was running for student body president right here on
this campus, near this building.

We made a papier-mâché Mickey Mouse head and rounded
out the uniform with a blue blazer, white pants, white turtle-

neck, and white gloves, and we started campaigning. We even had a ragtime band for our rallies. I remember it well. I was Mickey Mouse. It was a tough job, but I've never run away from a challenge. So there I was. A short, cocky protest candidate from Texas with a squeaky voice and giant ears— years ahead of Ross Perot!

And as a matter of fact, we did so well that one of the other candidates came up to me one day and tried to make a deal for my support. She asked me, "What do you want?"

I said, "More cheese, bigger holes, no mousetraps."

It was all a bit silly, maybe even cynical. But we had a lot of fun, we came in third, and we shook up campus politics.

And that turned out to be the beginning of a long journey in politics for me, a journey that quickly grew very serious, not so funny at all, as it passed through the antiwar struggle, the struggle for civil rights, and on into elective offices in the Colorado legislature and the mayor's office in Denver, and now to the position of Cabinet secretary for President Clinton.

Looking back, I can see this journey has taken me from cynicism and anger against government on to an idealism about what government can achieve when individuals are willing to get involved, take a stand, and try to make a difference. Now, after years in public office, and after what I hope are some genuine accomplishments, I still have that idealism, but I also have a new realism about the limitations of government action. This fascinating journey of understanding has brought me back tonight to Austin, and it even takes me back to my birthplace in South Texas.

Because these days, more than ever, I appreciate the values I learned from my parents as a child and here at UT as a young man. And I realize that deeply held values are the only true foundations we can build our lives on as individuals, as a nation, and as a society. As this whole journey from cynicism to idealism to realism comes home to basic values, I have a fresh sense of hope and renewal.

But as I talk to young Americans across our land, I don't often see much hope or any sense of renewal. What I feel instead is a current of pessimism, a sense of diminished opportunities. Many of you, like college graduates across the country, are deeply concerned about jobs and your futures and whether or not you'll be able to use your education, your skills, and your talents to the fullest. But there is something deeper than economic anxiety shaking our confidence.

Americans of all ages are chilled by statistics such as the 560 percent increase in crime over the last thirty years, the 400 percent rise in out-of-wedlock births, the quadrupling of divorces, the doubling of teen sucide rates, the gunplay in grade schools, the resurgence in heroin use, and the continuing plague of AIDS.

It is impossible to deny that our country has in many ways gone astray, that we face a crisis of true values. Tonight the eyes of Texas are upon you.

But in a real sense the eyes of people all over the world are upon your generation of Americans. Because it is the great task of your generation—and mine—to restore the American Dream, the promise that our country has always lived by, the promise of passing on a better way of life, a secure future, and a foundation of strong values. The whole world is watching us to see whether we will succeed or fail. Where will we stand? How will we handle this historic responsibility?

America is a community of shared values. America as a country has always been carried forward by its people and by our values, not by the government. Government can make good laws; it cannot make good people. Government may build a hospital, but we must visit the sick and comfort the dying. Government must build schools, good schools, but parents are the ultimate teachers. Government can build libraries and parks and gyms, but we must encourage the children of broken homes and mean streets to read and to play and to grow and not join gangs or do drugs.

Government can be a partner, but it is we, the people, taking up our responsibilities, living as best we can by high values, we are the only ones who can realize the possibility of this country and pass the best of America from generation to generation. Every one of us, if we will, can make a difference. So where will we stand?

America's history and our own experience prove that a single individual, brave enough to stand up for principle, can be the catalyst for enormous change. Forty years ago this week, in its famous *Brown* v. *Board of Education* ruling, our Supreme Court declared that school segregation was unconstitutional. But that Court's ruling alone didn't change America. People did, starting more than a year after the Supreme Court ruling, when one tired woman on her way home from work, a seamstress named Rosa Parks, refused to give up her seat in the whites-only section of a bus in Alabama. So Rosa Parks was arrested and taken to jail. But because she stood up for her civil rights, the great movement for civil rights for all Americans began in earnest.

Ten years later, with the passage of the Civil Rights and Voting Rights Act, the movement made up of millions of people finally put an end to legal segregation in this country. But someone had to stand up. Or take Cesar Chavez, fighting for the rights of migrant workers, a struggle that continues to this day. Time after time we've seen people take on battles that seemed too big to win. But they knew someone had to stand up. Bobby Kennedy knew that.

More than a generation ago, when South Africa's apartheid system was in its ugly prime, Senator Kennedy spoke to that country's young people. He told them: "Each of us can work to change a small portion of events and in the total of those acts will be written the history of a generation. It is from numberless acts of courage and belief that human history is shaped. Each time someone stands up for an ideal, or acts to improve the lot of others, or strikes out against injustice, then that person sends out a ripple of hope, and energy, and daring. These ripples build a current that can sweep away the mightiest walls of oppression and resistance."

Those were brave, idealistic words in 1966. But two weeks ago we saw Nelson Mandela take office as president of a new South Africa. President Mandela was behind bars, a political prisoner, when Bobby Kennedy spoke, but his victory makes Bobby Kennedy's idealistic words seem completely realistic, down-to-earth, full of common sense.

But what else was it but "numberless acts of courage and belief," coming from people just like us, that overcame apartheid?

What else was it but people brave enough to act who fueled our civil rights movement? Or toppled the Berlin Wall or started the movement toward peace in the Middle East?

All of these great moments in history, changes in human hearts and souls, changes brought about by people who refused to give in to doubt or pessimism, people who stood up and acted. Now it is our turn. And where do we stand?

I tell you tonight that if every American as privileged as we are would stand up and touch the life and raise the hopes of one young person, we would make giant strides toward binding up our nation's wounds, restoring faith in America's future, faith in ourselves, and, most importantly, faith in our values. I say "most importantly" because everything we achieve—everything—depends fundamentally on the values we believe in, live by, and pass on. It is our values, our belief in work and family above all that sustain America's society and our political and economic structure.

For me, these values began as child and grew in my teenage years, sweeping cotton dust from the floor of my father's office, pouring concrete in construction jobs in the summers, shoveling sorghum in a grain elevator. Here at UT I washed dishes at Kingsolving Girls dormitory and cooked hamburgers on Nineteenth Street. They were pretty tasty burgers too, at least when I made them. These weren't dream jobs. But my friends and I took jobs like these because we had learned the value of work, like all our values, from our parents. My father and mother, who are here tonight, put six children through college, saving and sacrificing. Instead of spending on themselves, they invested in us. Over time they raised three lawyers, an accountant, an assistant high school principal, and a teacher. Unfortunately two of them became Aggies.

They taught us, mostly by example, to work and sacrifice, to be honest, to believe in God, to love our country, and to take all the opportunities America gave us and meet all the responsibilities it asked of us. Now that I am a parent myself, I wonder whether I can ever meet the high standards that they set for me and live up to the values they lived by.

Soon many of you will become parents. You too will have to make choices and real commitments to your families and to your country. And, my friends, let me tell you that these times cry out for us to act, to take a stand. We cannot afford to be cynical or blindly idealistic. We need a healthy realism about what government can do and should do. And a willingness to then engage ourselves personally in the things government cannot do.

It is up to my generation, and now yours, to meet a challenge that every other generation of Americans before us has faced and met: the challenge of passing on a better America to those who come after us. This very night this challenge, like a torch, is being passed on to you. We need you. We're proud of you.

And if you take up this responsibility joyfully, if you love your families and broaden your reach to care for neighbors and strangers and for our country, then you will send out ripples of hope that will sustain America for your children and their children after them. I know there are a lot of people like that here tonight. Those who have loved you and believed in you and helped you make it here tonight, people who are counting on you.

You can make a difference. You can change the world. Because you are the difference. You are the world.

With your hearts and hands and minds joining us, I do believe that this generation will show the whole world that America's best days are yet to come. And that the Amercan Dream is much too young to die.

Toni Morrison

Sarah Lawrence College
May 27, 1988

Toni Morrison is one of America's most treasured writers,
teachers, and critics. Among her many honors are a Pulitzer
Prize for Beloved *in 1987 and a Nobel Prize in literature in*
1993 for The Bluest Eye, *which was originally published in*
1970. This thought-provoking speech has been referred to as
one of the most memorable commencement addresses ever given
to a graduating class at Sarah Lawrence College.

By the reputation of your faculty and the alumni of this college, I guess that your education here has not been idle or
irrelevant. I would guess that it has been serious, and I would
like by what I say to approach the seriousness of your tenure
here. So, what do you say to the Sarah Lawrence Class of
'88? The last time I did this, I think, was in 1984, and that
year was so fraught with the symbolism and the tension that
Mr. Wells had projected on to it, it was difficult not to make
it the subject of every speech. And I still don't know what
really might be of value to any graduating class four years
after 1984. Well, obviously, I must make some reference to
the future—how sparkling it can be—provided, of course,
that it exists. If only the possibility of actually killing time
was not a real one. Real because if we want it that way, we
can arrange things so that there will be no one left to imagine
or even remember that human invention time. Its absence has
been thinkable during the whole of your lives. I would talk
about the future. If only it were a rolled carpet that you just

had to kick to see it unfurl limitlessly before your feet. But then there is some requirement to talk about responsibility. I am addressing, after all, bright, industrious, accomplished people who are about to shoulder the very considerable weight of educated adulthood. So there should be some mention of responsibility. The need for and the risk in assuming the burden of one's own life and, in the course of that, assuming the care of another. A child, a friend, a mate, a parent, an acquaintance, even perhaps a stranger. Shouldn't I also talk about goodness, ethical choices? I ought to. Since goodness is not only better and good for you, it's really more interesting, more complicated, more demanding, less predictable, more adventuresome than its opposite. Evil really is boring. Sensational perhaps but not interesting. It's a kind of low-level activity that needs masses, or singularity, or screams, or screeching headlines to even get any attention for itself, and goodness doesn't need anything.

Then how can I leave out happiness? How can I omit the secret ingredients, the combination of which will invite, if not guarantee, it? A little parity, a bit of daring, some luck, and a great deal of self-regard. Then life is bountiful, and one is loved and lovable.

Now that's a good program. The future, responsibility, goodness. I'd like to do all that, except for that last one, happiness. It makes me uneasy. Besides, I am not interested in your happiness. First of all, I'm not sure it's all it's cracked up to be. I know of course that its pursuit, if not its achievement, is a legal one amended into the Constitution. I know that whole industries are designed to help you identify, attain, and feel it. One more article of clothing? Or the ultimate telephone. The best-appointed apartment, a boat, an instantly timeless camera taking hundreds of shots meant to outlast the ages. The fastest diet, or the best of all the perfect ice creams with all of the pleasures of sugar and cream and none of their dangers. I know also that happiness has been the real, covert target of your labors here, your choices perhaps of companions, the profession that you wish to enter, and I do really want you to have it, because you deserve it; everybody does. And I hope it continues or comes effortlessly, quickly, always. Still, I'm not interested in it—not yours, and not mine and not anybody's. I don't think we can afford it anymore. I don't think it delivers the goods. But most important, it's getting in the way of everything worth doing. Now, there was a time, actually, for most of the history of the human race in which to contemplate and to strive for happiness was not just critical, it was necessarily compelling. But I think focusing on it now has gotten quite out of hand. It's become a bankrupt idea. The vocabulary of which is frightening. Money and things and protection and control and speed and more and more and more.

I'd like to think about and substitute something else for its search, for its pursuit. Something urgent. Something neither the world nor you can continue without. I am assuming you have already been trained to think, to have an intelligent encounter with problem solving. It's certainly what you will be expected to do. But I want to talk about the step before that. The preamble to problem solving. I want to talk about the activity you are always warned against as being wasteful, impractical, hopeless. I want to talk about dreaming. Not the activity of the sleeping brain but rather the activity of an awake and alert one. Not idle, wishful speculation but engaged, directed daytime vision. Entrance into another space. Someone else's situation, sphere, projection, if you like. By dreaming, the self permits intimacy with the other without the risk of being the other. And this intimacy that comes from pointed imagining, should precede all of our decision making, all of our cause mongering and our action. We are in a mess, you know, and we have to get out.

And I believe it is the archaic definition of the word "dreaming" that will say this. That definition is to envision a series of images of unusual vividness, clarity, order, and significance. Unusual vividness, clarity, order, and significance. If we undertake that kind of dreaming, we can avoid complicating what is simple and simplify what is complicated. We would avoid substituting slogans like national will for national perception. What kind of national will? Informed? Uninformed? Obstinate? South African national will? Nineteen forty Germany's national will? We can avoid hanging on to destructive theses simply because we developed them half a century ago. We can avoid comic book solutions to biblical problems in nuclear times. We should visualize, imagine, dream up, and enter the other before we presume to solve their problems or ours. We might as well dream the world as it ought to be.

Imagine—why don't we?—what would it actually feel like to live in a world, imagine what it would be like not to be living in a world loaded with zero life weapons. Manned by people willing to loose them, develop them or store them for money, for power, for information, for data, but never, ever for your life, and never, ever for mine. What would it be like to live in a world where the solutions of serious, learned people to practically every big problem was not to kill somebody? Narcotics trade—whom shall we kill or lock up? Disease—whom shall we let die or lock up? Self, ruled by a neighboring or even distant country—whom shall we slaughter? Famine—what is an acceptable death rate? Unemployment, homeless—what is the tolerable starvation rate? Too many babies by all of the wrong mothers. Too many people living too long. Even our goodwill is couched in killing. We are asked to give millions of dollars to feed the children until they are fourteen, at which point we are forced to pay billions to blow their brains out if they make demands in their own interests but not in ours. Are their deaths not timely enough for us? They'll die anyway. We all will. All of the babies, all the elderly, all the fettered, all the unenfranchised, all the ill, all the idle—just like us. Maybe after, maybe before, maybe even because we will all be together by and by. . . .

If that is the consequence of sophisticated twentieth-century thinking, our expert problem solving, then we need to step back and refine the process that precedes it, experimental, intimate, ranging daylight vision that is not ashamed to dream or to visualize the other. Envision what it would be like to know that your comfort, your fun, your safety are not based on the deprivation of another.

It is possible that we are committed to outmoded paradigms, to moribund thinking that has not been preceded by nor even dappled by dreams. It's possible, but now it's necessary, absolutely necessary because if you don't feed the poor, they will have no choice but to eat you, and the manner of their eating will be as varied as it is ferocious. They'll eat your houses, your neighborhood, your city, sleep in your lobbies, in your lanes, your gardens, your intersections. They'll eat your revenue because there will never be enough prisons and wards and hospitals and welfare hotels to accommodate them. And in their search for that kind of happiness I mentioned that makes me so uneasy, the things and control and speed and more, in that pursuit they may end up eating your children, render them as stunned and terrified as they already are desperate. For the sleeping life narcotics can offer, we may already have lost the creative intelligence of two thirds of a new generation as of this moment and lost it to a poisoned and violent sleep. A torpor so brutal that you can't wake from it for fear you'll remember it. A sleep of such numbed recklessness it turns our own wakefulness to dread.

It is possible to live without defending property or surrendering it. We will never live that way unless our thinking, our problem solving, is shot through with dreams. And it's necessary now, it's necessary now because if you don't educate the unschooled with the very best you have, if you don't give them the help, give them the courtesy, the respect *you* had in becoming educated, then they will educate themselves, and the things they will teach you and the things they will learn may destabilize all you know. And by "education" I don't mean hobbling the mind but liberating it. By "education" I don't mean passing on monologues but engaging in dialogues, listening sometimes, assuming sometimes that I have a history, that I have a language, a view, an idea, a specificity. Assuming that what I know may be useful, may enhance what you know, may extend or even complete it. My memory is as necessary to yours as yours is necessary to mine.

Before we look for a usable past, we ought to know all of it. Before we start reclaiming a legacy, we ought to know exactly what that legacy is, all of it, and where it came from. In the business of education there are no minorities. There is only minor thinking because if education requires tuition but no meaning, it's going to be about nothing other than careers. If it's about nothing other than defining and husbanding beauty, isolating goods, and making sure enrichments are the privilege of a few, if that's what education is, then it can be stopped in the sixth grade, where everybody learned it, or the sixth century, where everybody invested in it. Because the rest is just reinforcement if that's all that education is about. The function of twentieth-century education must be to produce humane human beings. To refuse to continue to produce generation after generation of people trained to make expedient decisions rather than humane ones.

Well, what would it be like to live without that putrefying hatred that we have been told and taught was inevitable, natural among human beings? Inevitable, natural after a presence of five million years. After recording ourselves for four thousand years. We haven't thought of anything better than that! And which one of us was born that way? Which one of us prefers it that way? Hating, or grabbing, or despising? Racism is a scholarly pursuit, and it always has been. It's not gravity or the ocean tides; it's the invention of our minor thinkers, our minor leaders, our minor scholars, and our major entrepreneurs. And it can be uninvented, deconstructed. Its annihilation begins with just dreaming about, visualizing its absence. Lose it. If it can't be lost at once, or just by saying so, then behave as if it were. Behave as if our free life depended on it because it does. If I spend my life despising you because of your race, or your class, or your religion, then I become your slave. If you spend yours hating me for similar reasons, it's because you have become my slave. I have your energy; I have your fear; I have your intellect; I can determine where you live, how you live, what your work is. I can determine your definition of excellence, and I can set the limits to your ability to love, which means I will have shaped your life. That is the gift of your hatred: You are mine.

Well, now, you may be asking yourself, "What is all of this? I can't save the world. What about my life?" you ask. "I didn't come here for this. I didn't even ask to come here. I didn't ask to be born." Didn't you? I put it to you that you did. You not only asked to be born, you insisted on your life. That's why you're here. There's no other reason. It's too easy not to have been born, and now that you're here, you have to do something. Something you respect, don't you? Your parents may have wanted you, but they did not dream you up. You did that. I'm just urging you to continue the dream you started, because dreaming is not irresponsible. It's first order, human business. It's not entertainment, you know. It's work. When Martin Luther King said, "I have a dream," he wasn't playing; he was serious. When he imagined it, envisioned, created it in his own mind, it began. Now we have to dream it too and give it the heft and stretch and longevity it deserves, but don't let anybody convince you this is the way the world is and therefore must be. It must be the way it ought to be. Full employment is possible and desirable. Positing a work force of 20 to 30 percent of the population in the future is yearning greed, not inevitable economics. All public schools can be hospitable, welcoming, safe learning environments. Nobody, no teacher, no student, prefers mindlessness. And I'm happy to say, that such environments are rapidly being considered and built in otherwise devastated areas. Appetites for self-murder can be eradicated. No addict or suicide wants to be one. Enemies, racists, nations, they can too live together. Even I, in the last forty years, have seen five deadly national enemies become warm, mutually supporting friends. At least four national friends have become four national enemies. And it doesn't take forty years to witness that. Anybody over eight years old has already witnessed the expedient, commercial, almost whimsical nature of national friendships. I have seen resources committed to the disenfranchised, to the discredited, to the merely unlucky, and before we could reap the harvest of those resources, before legislation put in place could work—what, twenty years?—it was disassembled. It's like stopping the Union in 1796 because there were problems. Like building the Tappan Zee halfway across the Hudson and then saying, "We can't get there from here."

That determined commitment must be redreamed, rebought, reactivated by me and you. Otherwise, as the nationalisms and racisms solidify, as coasts and villages become and remain sources of turmoil and dispute, as eagles and doves cover over the remaining sources of the overall wealth of the earth, as guns and gold and cocaine topple grain, technology, and medicine to win first place in world trade, if these things go on, we will end up with a world not worth sharing or even dreaming about.

What I mean to say is we are already life chosen by ourselves, humans, and as far as we know, there aren't any more. We are the moral inhabitants of the galaxy. Why trash that magnificent obligation after working so hard in the womb to assume it? You will be in positions that matter. Positions in which you can decide the nature and quality of other people's lives. Your errors may be irrevocable. So when you enter those places of trust and power, dream a little before you think and solve. So, your thoughts, your solutions, your directions, choices about who lives and who doesn't, who flourishes and who doesn't, will be worth the very sacred life that you already chose to live.

You are not helpless and you're not heartless, and you have time. Thank you.

IV

You Will Succeed

A .300 hitter would hit his pitch every time, but as often as not when the .280 hitter would get his pitch, he'd foul it off. The same difference seems to be true of most of what we attempt in life...when the time comes just two things matter. How well prepared we are to seize the moment. And having the courage to take our best swing.

—Hank Aaron

Garrison Keillor

Gettysburg College
May 17, 1987

Garrison Keillor is a broadcaster best known as the creator and host of A Prairie Home Companion, *the radio program centered on the events of the fictional town of Lake Wobegon, Minnesota. The show, which ran on more than two hundred stations on the American Public Radio network, received a Peabody Award in 1981 and a Grammy in 1987. Keillor retired in 1987, then returned to the airwaves in 1989 with* American Radio Company of the Air. *In this address he discusses the joys and trials of becoming parents.*

I bring you greetings from Lake Wobegon, to all of you in the German branch of the Lutheran Church—we pray for you daily without ceasing. It's a great pleasure for all of us on this platform to be part of your day—the Class of '87. And to be here as witnesses at this grave and solemn moment in your lives.

When I graduated from college, I sat about where you are and watched a candidate for summa cum laude honors walk up the stairs to be recognized, and step on the inside hem of his gown. And walk all the way up the inside of it. It was something that we all remembered, who saw it, as an object lesson in how talent and intelligence might fare in this world. And some of us had tears in our eyes as we saw it.

What is a solemn occasion for you, however, is a kind of humorous one for me, because I have arrived at the humorous age at which my friends, and people whom I went around with in Lake Wobegon, are now old enough to have children your age graduating from college. People whom I saw in their youthful and reckless moments are now looking at the backs of your heads as you get set to commence: A boy whom I drove around town with a '57 pink Oldsmobile with terrific chrome and a horn—an air horn—that when you pulled the wire under the dash, it made the sound of a cow mooing; a girl whom I danced with outdoors one summer night at a party, to music of Little Richard and Elvis and the Everlys. We danced outside the grass in the dark because we were brought up strict—to believe that dancing was carnal and therefore wrong. But whatever it was indoors, it was even more the same outside. It was an exciting event, dancing in the dark in your stocking feet, on the grass.

And now these two friends and others whom I knew are the parents of some rather tall people. And distinguished scholars. This is the third commencement I was invited to this spring; at the others not to speak but to attend, and if not to attend, to send gifts. And so today I would like to speak in behalf of your parents, if I may—and I will. And can. When I saw how much tuition was here, I think they're entitled to it.

It's a great surprise and a great privilege in life to know people whom you've known since before they existed and back when they were theoretical. And even before that. To have known their parents when their parents were contemplating having children with somebody else. Ponder that for a moment. Some of us were around when you were without a name. When you were—when you were just sort of a notion late one night. It's a privilege to see you grow up and come along.

I want to tell you on behalf of your parents that you did not interrupt anything important for us. Like our childhood, for example. We were children back in the 1950s, which was a grim and a nervous time, and were glad to be rid of it. And you were the first sign that we were. Nostalgia for the 1950s is done by people with poor memories, and I feel better the farther from it I get. Ever so often you may hear hints from your parents of things they might have done if they hadn't had you. Such as have a lifestyle, for example, or write poetry, or write fiction, or work on their backhand, or travel, and be more interesting people. But we don't mean it. You were the best thing—one of the best things—that came along and happened to us.

If you are the first child, you are one of the two most amazing things that happened to your parents. A couple. And if you came later in the family, you were just as amazing as that, but without all of the worry and the fears. Not that you weren't worried over. You have been worried over religiously. Your breathing was checked many, many nights when you were little tiny, tiny people, the size of a bread loaf. One parent or the other got up late in the night to come in and see if your backside was moving up and down. We have worried about stepping on you; we've worried about what we fed you; we've worried about everything that could be worried about—and a little bit more.

I have a son who's about your age. And I found him once, when he was a little boy, chewing on something that turned out to be part of a rodent. It was a mouse that had died of rat poison. It's a wonder, in our drive to the doctor's, that we weren't all killed. I just cite that as a mild example of how we've worried about you and how we still do, even today—your parents and I. We're wondering if you have handkerchiefs—on you. We're wondering if you're fully dressed under these robes.

You were an amazing event in our lives. You were truly, truly amazing. You were a great stroke of wonderful, wonderful luck. When I was a young man before I had children,

I was a sad man. I had a grudge against the world and what it had done to me, and my parents, and what they owed me. And when this child came along, and it turned out to be a difficult birth, and we sat with fears that this child would be born dead, and when he finally appeared, that melancholy part of my life was over. The book shut on it, and I entered another life, the life of a parent, which I think almost every parent far, far prefers.

Parents are cheerful and forward-looking people. We are inherently hopeful. And we looked forward to the time when you walked, and to your first words, and to your first sentences. Some of you, we're still looking forward to your first good paragraphs, but we're hopeful.

We are inherently looking out for the best. We are terribly proud of you, and we always were, although we've tried to be tasteful about it. And not to constantly talk about you while you're in our presence. If this were not commencement at Gettysburg College, but instead were visiting day at the state prison, and we were here to bring you fruit and some magazines, we would still be proud of you—though we're grateful for the difference. A life behind bars is something that's been contemplated by every parent.

And it's not that we didn't have faith in you. It's that we lacked faith in ourselves as parents. Being a parent is not something that people ever feel confident or secure about. When you were tiny children, we started to read about tremendous advances in prenatal education. And when you got a little bit older, we started reading great books about early childhood and fantastic things parents can do. We've always been a step behind in bringing you up. You came a little bit too late for the computer boom—just a little late. You should have had one when you were two or three years old. It would have changed your life and made you better people, and we know it, and we feel sorry that we couldn't have given it to you. Back when you were two or three years old, computers were the size of dining room tables. And they cost a parent's annual salary. But that doesn't change the fact that we feel bad for not having given it to you.

We wanted to bring you up with information about sex that we never had. Our parents only told us that if we listened to rock 'n' roll, we would have babies, and they were right. You are them. We wanted you to grow up knowing more, and to have complete information, and to think of sex as being natural and good. And then, when you first showed interest, we were alarmed at how young you were. And so much we haven't talked about it as much as we should've, and—so I'll just pass over that section of my speech.

We're terribly proud of you, and to see you here, in some ways relieved that you didn't have to live our lives all over again. It's a sobering thing to bring a child into this world, an act of vanity at the beginning, to produce somebody who is just exactly like yourself—too much so. And then the pride that we have in you now, to see you as you take steps toward independence, and to walk through that door which you have to do, so you can forgive us, and then you can walk back in sometime, and something else will happen. We can be friends of some sort.

Your parents and I were not the members of the Love Generation, the flower children, we were just a few years too early for that. Those were other people who talked about love. We were more practical. I'm proud of my generation, which seems to me to have been brave, and loud, and funny. And most of all, we're proud of having produced you. We have high hopes for you—high hopes. And speaking in be-half of your parents, I want to tell you how much we love all of you.

God bless you—God bless you as much as God blessed us when he sent you along. Thank you so much, and now go and do good.

Andy Rooney

Colgate University
May 19, 1996

*Veteran television correspondent, writer, and producer Andy
Rooney is best known for his pointed and humorous
commentary on "A Few Minutes with Andy Rooney,"
which has appeared weekly on the television newsmagazine
60 Minutes for the last twenty years. Among his many career
highlights, Rooney has won three Emmys for his essays, six
Writers Guild awards for Best Script (more than anyone in
television), and a Peabody Award for Mr. Rooney Goes to
Washington, a special he wrote, produced, and narrated for
CBS News. A member of the Class of 1942 at Colgate,
Rooney returned to his alma mater in 1996 to discuss the
trappings of technology and the value of friendship.*

It's strange for me, being here at this graduation ceremony.
The surroundings here at Colgate are so familiar to me, but
my relationship to them is so different.

I am somewhere in between feeling important to be speaking to you on such a significant day in your lives and ridiculous to be standing here in this costume. I, at least, unlike
some of you, probably, have something on under this besides
my Jockey shorts.

You can be proud of yourselves for having graduated from
Colgate. Five years ago I said that Colgate was a better college then than it was when I was here. Today I believe it's

a better college than it was five years ago. By the standard I use to measure academic excellence, you can't argue with me.

I judge the academic excellence of a college in inverse ratio to the success of its football team. By those standards Colgate is one of the outstanding academic institutions in America. That's what we get for letting the students play.

To tell you the truth, I wouldn't mind having us win a few games, but I'm pleased that Colgate is no Nebraska, no Miami. Anytime a college wins more than half its games over a long period of time against opponents in comparable institutions, it's probably cheating. Obviously what we have to do in the next few years in order to win half our games is cheat a little.

There are ten thousand things I'd like to tell you, and I've had to choose just a few. If living a happy life gives a person the right to advise others on how to live their lives, then I am eminently qualified.

I still get up at five-thirty every morning because I like my life so much that I hate to waste any of it by sleeping more than is necessary. I wish I could follow the same rule by not eating any more than is necessary to sustain my body.

University marshal Bill Oostenink leads his last processional. I guess first and most important I'd like to try to convince you how good life can be if you don't already know it. There are some really terrible times ahead for you—everyone has them—but life, all in all, can be spectacularly good. If this were not so, none of us my age and older would be so desperately trying to fend off our impending demise.

One of the things you have to face, though, is the unpleasant fact that you will not ever arrive at any condition of life with which you are totally satisfied and happy. It seems unfortunate, but it's true, that to experience real happiness, you first, or occasionally anyway, have to be unhappy. So you're going to be unhappy sometimes. Just accept it as part of the process. Ambition and satisfaction are at war. If you're ambitious, you aren't satisfied, and if you're satisfied, you aren't ambitious.

Most of us are plagued by ambition. It's one of the best and the worst things about us. There is no point of success we achieve where we say, "That's it. That's all of anything I want. I don't want to be any happier, I don't want to have a bigger house, a better car. I don't need more respect from my friends."

You're never going to get to the point where you're content. I've been successful and it's satisfying, but the best parts of my life are the small day-to-day pleasures—a drink of cold water, the newspaper in the driveway, beating someone away from a traffic light. I take more enjoyment from sitting at my desk writing than I take from the money it brings in. That's a good thing because I write every day but I get paid only once every two weeks.

If I could influence you at all with what I am saying here today—and I realize that a speech like this is just an obligatory formality that will have no effect whatsoever—I know the direction in which I'd head you if I could. I'd try to get you to face what's good about life and what's bad about life with intelligence, knowledge, and logic.

I wish you would face the unknown without trying to explain the inexplicable with man-made answers and superstitious nonsense. I wish you could look directly at the world and its problems and at your own life and try to solve those problems with reason.

The tendency people have—even very smart people—to fool themselves and turn their backs on what their brains tell them is constantly depressing to me. I have great faith in the strength of intelligence and reason even though I may have a limited amount of either. We have to believe that honest and educated inspection of all our problems is the best way to live successfully. There are a lot of people who don't believe that. They prefer not to face the truth about anything.

All this inability to face the truth doesn't make them bad people; it comes from modesty. A sense of inadequacy they have. They feel that if everything they are and everything they're going to become in this world depends on their own ability, then they're afraid that they're in trouble. They don't think they're capable enough to do it right. If, on the other hand, their success and happiness depends on hoping and praying, getting help from the government and maybe winning the lottery, then they aren't nervous. They feel their destiny is in better hands than their own.

Well, I don't think it is, and I hope you can be persuaded that it is not.

Even though I believe living with your brain is the best course, I have to tell you that most of what you learned in college will be of absolutely no use to you whatsoever. College is actually not much more than a place where parents who can afford it store their children for four years because they can't stand having them around the house while they age.

The good thing about having an education is that it will be a lifelong consolation to you. It will be a pleasure every day. It isn't what an education does for you that makes getting one worthwhile; it's having one. Doing something with it isn't the end product. Being educated is an end in itself. It sets you apart from most of the people on the planet.

I got an education at Colgate that's been a little help, but it was a spotty one. As I recall, you were on the dean's list if you had two As and a B, and you were on probation if you had two Es. When I was here, I distinguished myself one semester by being the only student simultaneously on the dean's list and probation.

I know many of you are worried about what comes next. I understand that. I don't know how anyone ever gets a job. It seems so impossible when you're setting out. In a sense you're freshmen all over again. Whatever you do, I hope you set out to make something. I mean that in the broadest sense. We need doctors, not medical plans; mechanics, not car salesmen; farmers, not frozen food packagers.

You have an education; now you have to see how much of it works. You'll find, not much. I know that in your first job you can't set out to improve the world or remake mankind, and it's always foolish for graduation speakers to suggest any grand idea like this. If you want to help mankind, find a job you like and do it as well as you can. We idolize people who take on some noble cause and devote their lives to it, and I admire them too, but not many of us can do that, and short of that, the most help you can be to yourself and everyone else is to live well. If you take care of yourself and your family and provide that one unit of well-being in the world, you'll have done your part. If you can do more than that, great.

There's no harm dreaming of something bigger, though. Wouldn't it be fun to start a company, not with the intention of getting rich, but with the idea of making some good product and providing a lot of people with a job? Why couldn't goodness be the goal of selfish ambition, rather than money? Couldn't a capable executive make providing happiness for other people his motivating force?

It's my opinion that whatever you decide to do, your fate is in your own hands. The idea that man's fate is predetermined is nonsense. *Que será será* is the philosophy of a person who doesn't have enough self-confidence to put his life in his own hands.

I wouldn't deny that some very small incident can change the course of your life in some major way, but for the most part it's the manner and intelligence—or lack of intelligence—with which you make a thousand small decisions throughout the day, beginning with tying your shoelace, that takes you where you're going and fills your life with good or bad years.

It's apparent that successful people are more apt to think that luck isn't much of a factor than unsuccessful people, but it is nonetheless true. If you don't think knowledge and intelligence are the best tools for building a good life, look at the world. See where literacy, thought, and expression are greatest, and then look at the areas where literacy and freedom of thought are lowest. In every case the standard of living is highest among literate people. The more literate, the higher the standard.

I hope you can keep from measuring your success strictly in terms of how much money you make. The government regularly issues manufacturing statistics that are considered "good" by Wall Street if they are high, and "bad" if they are low. The government is disinterested in—or doesn't know how to measure—the quality of things manufactured. The government doesn't know how to judge the total effect that the things manufactured have on our lives.

It doesn't matter that sometimes the things manufactured are simpleminded toys or weapons designed to kill people. If someone makes money from their manufacture, the government puts them in the "good" column. Production was up. Forget that the product made was something that made us fat or sick or wasted our time or in some other way had a negative effect on our lives. Forget that while production was up, quality declined.

There's no question that all the great technological advances make it easier for people to live and eat without spending full-time working to support themselves. We have a lot more free time, but we don't seem to have found anything good to do with it. I don't even know why free time or vacation is held in such high regard. Personally I enjoy working in my free time.

No matter how technical your job may be, I hope you don't lose track of how satisfying physical labor is—or forget that you can use your brains lifting too. Blue-collar workers no longer wear shirts with blue collars, and white-collar workers are very apt to wear blue denim shirts. The lines are blurred.

I hope you learn how to do something besides your job. Play a musical instrument, paint a picture, make a chocolate cake. I avoid the word "hobby" because that has an inconsequential connotation. Hobbies are fine, but you ought to be better than a hobbyist.

If I had three lives to live, I'd be a carpenter or a cabinetmaker in one of them because I find woodworking so satisfying. I think there's some evidence that more people with college educations are doing manual jobs too. Brain and muscle are a great combination.

There's a sign in the service area of the Ford dealership across the street from my office that says LABOR: $80 AN HOUR. An eight-hour day, eight times eighty, times five, times fifty-two. How many of you would settle on that? And who says someone who fixes cars or builds a rock wall can't go home at night and read a book?

I'm constantly impressed by how little the high-tech inventions we think of as progress have really helped. When I don't have anything else to think about, I think about whether all of mankind cumulatively is happier, less happy, or just about the same in relation to happiness as it was a hundred or two thousand years ago before electric lights, automobiles, airplanes, television, or Diet Pepsi.

No instrument has ever been invented to measure the happiness waves emanating from thousand-year-old skeletons.

And just as I question whether people over the world were any happier before they had all these toys, I doubt we're any smarter than people were a thousand years before.

No instrument has been invented that measures the smart waves coming from mummies either. It probably took as much intelligence to invent the slingshot as the atomic bomb. You have to consider the possibility that technology hasn't really improved the human condition overall or made us any happier either. Are we getting more work done with all the time we save on the job? Not that I notice.

It was assumed that computers would reduce the amount of paper we consume. Computers are chewing into stacks of stationery like no amount of carbon paper or Xerox machines ever did. Has our ability to communicate with each other on the telephone and the Internet brought communities, families, friends closer together? I don't think so.

We've built ribbons of major highways everywhere. We've paved America to relieve traffic on smaller roads. Is traffic reduced anywhere you know of? Have automated tellers made lines shorter at the bank? Now that you pump your own gas a lot of places, have they reduced the price of a gallon of gas because they don't have to pay someone to pump it? Did you get better marks because it was easier to find information you needed on a computer than it used to be to find it in a book?

President Clinton said in a speech in New Hampshire that most of the work in the world that used to be physical labor is now technological. Maybe. I'm skeptical. I use a computer, but I can't help remembering that behind every technological device there is someone who makes something or does something with his or her hands. It's fine to talk about how much easier it is to distribute information and to communicate with each other, but if no one makes anything, writes anything, or has any interesting ideas, what difference does it make how easy it is to communicate? Communicate what?

We desperately need to concentrate on the content of what's being communicated, rather than the method of transportation. The idea of E-mail is terrific. The thought contained in most messages sent over it is close to zero. When I'm working, my computer beeps when I get an E-mail message. Last week I was deep into writing something and the damn thing started beeping. I stopped what I was doing, went to MAIL, hit some keys, waited, and pretty soon the message came up. The father of a technician I never heard of at CBS had died, the message said, and there would be a service Friday at a funeral home on Eighty-first Street and Madison Avenue. Well, it's a tragedy for the technician and his father, but hundreds of thousands of people I don't know die every day and I don't want to be advised individually on my computer about each one. There isn't time to be sad for the whole world.

The Internet is a garbage dump of monstrous proportions. I go to the dump in my hometown often enough to know there's some great stuff there, but I'm not interested in spending my time sorting through it. A few weeks ago I saw a guy throwing away two perfectly good IBM electric typewriters. I've gone to the dump on the Internet and have yet to find anything worth the time I spent. I've never found anything as good as those two old IBM typewriters.

The intensification of our ability to transmit information has exceeded the mind's ability to take it in too. Do I know more than my grandfather knew because there is more available for me to know? Afraid not. Do you know more useful things than I know because during your learning years you had available to you the great resources of computers? I've talked to a few of you today, and I don't want to be insulting, but if you have vast knowledge in your head, you did a very good job of not making me feel inferior by hiding it from me.

I use my Lexis-Nexis, but it's not magic. Wednesday I spent forty-five minutes looking for something on my computer. I finally gave up, went one flight upstairs to the CBS library, and found what I wanted in a book in three minutes. I worry about everyone taking their facts from just a few sources, which is happening with computers. Will we end up with one big reference pool so that everyone goes to the same place for information and no new information from the past ever turns up?

My friend Harry Reasoner once gave me some good advice about commencement addresses. He said, "You can start out funny, but you should end up sad." I have a sad thought to end with today.

Something that has surprised and dismayed me is what happens to friends. You'll find that by the time you've reached my age, you've made more friends than you have time to keep. It seems unfair and wrong, but it's true. I had fifty reasonably close friends when I was in college here at Colgate. Seven were killed in World War II, but over the years I kept in touch with about ten of them. I didn't lose touch with the others because we no longer liked each other; we lost track of each other because there wasn't time enough in life to be friends with everyone you felt friendly towards. Fortunately there isn't time to hate everyone you don't like either.

But that's the big reason this is a sweet-and-sour day for you. It's sweet because you've gained a major objective in your life; it's sad because as I speak, you're seeing many friends for the last time.

And that's all the sad stuff I'm going to say. It hasn't been a long speech, I know that, but I've been in the audience during a lot of commencement addresses and when people commented about them after they were over, I don't ever recall hearing anyone say, "It was good, but it was too short."

I hope you'd feel good to know how honored I am to have been asked to speak to you.

Patrick Stewart

Pomona College
May 14, 1995

*A classically trained actor and member of the Royal
Shakespeare Company, Patrick Stewart has appeared in
numerous stage and screen productions, but he is perhaps best
known for his television role as Captain Jean-Luc Picard,
commander of the* Starship Enterprise *on* Star Trek: The
Next Generation. *The students of Pomona College undertook
a massive petition campaign requesting Stewart as their
commencement speaker, and he obliged them with a humorous
and emotional speech.*

President [Peter] Stanley, distinguished faculty and trustees,
fellow honorees, ladies and gentlemen, boys and girls, and
graduating Class of 1995. Now, I don't mean by that that
you are not ladies and gentlemen. Or indeed boys and girls.

Before the thrill and the emotion of this event utterly over-
whelms me, and like Caliban in *The Tempest,* I forget my
own meaning and gabble like a thing brutish, I must at once
address myself specifically and directly to this graduating student body, for it is this group of people who initiated the
invitation that has brought me here today. And I understood
only this morning that apparently I was the result of an active
writing campaign. You should know that during the past few
months in conversations with President Stanley and Professor
[Martha] Andreson they have reminded me of this from time
to time, it being clearly important to them that I should feel
this direct connection with you, the student body. And so, to

you, ladies and gentlemen, a very deeply felt thank-you. You are giving me indeed a day to remember and an honor for which I shall always be proud. Claremont and Pomona College will always have the very warmest place in my heart.

And now, given the dignity and solemnity of this occasion, it behooves me to come clean. I have a confession to make. I stand here almost a virgin. "Now pause here, Patrick" [as if reading from his speech]. Is it possible to be almost a virgin? Well, I am sure that there are those better qualified than I to meditate upon that subject and you'll be reassured to hear, I'm sure, that I'm speaking only figuratively. This is only my second graduation ceremony ever. And when I say "mine," I don't mean "mine," because this is in fact the only one in which I've actually been a participant. And to those of you who are at this moment reeling with shock, let me confirm that I never went to Starfleet Academy, that I never sat at the feet of the groundsperson Bootby, and I wouldn't know a space-time continuum or a warp core breach if they got into bed with me.

The first was when my son Daniel graduated three years ago from Cal Arts. A very different kind of commencement than this, for certainly at that time the emphasis there was on individual inventiveness and creativity in each particular student. My son, as a public gesture of his transformation from English jacketed and tied public schoolboy to California graduate, dressed in a Hawaiian shirt and Bermuda shorts. Four young men arrived in a fire engine to receive their degrees. But the most enterprising young man had concealed himself under the platform the night before. On the announcement of his name, he cut his way out through the stage floor with a chain saw. And that has been my only firsthand experience on graduation day.

It was a momentous day in my family when Daniel graduated. There he stood, Bachelor of Fine Arts, the first member of my family to receive a degree. It was as significant for me as it would, under any other circumstances, if he had been the first member of the family to read or write. I was tremendously proud and somewhat in awe of him. And not surprisingly. I, his father, had completed my formal education at the age of fifteen years and two days, the minimum age then required by the state of England at which schooling could cease. But unknown to me, I already represented a stage in intellectual development in my family. Years later, when I became interested in genealogy, and I was researching my ancestors, I found in the records office in Somerset House in London the marriage certificate of my great-grandparents, and where my maternal great-grandmother, Elizabeth Mountain, was to sign her name, there was merely a cross, an *X*. Elizabeth Mountain was illiterate and could only make her mark. Upon that same document her profession was described as "female laborer."

Ah, yes, I can already hear the murmurings and mutterings behind me [referring to the faculty sitting behind him]. "What is this? Are we honoring someone who is unqualified? Are we bestowing distinction on the unworthy?" Well, materially, yes, you are. But in granting me the singular and most distinguished honor, you are persuading me that I am a minuscule detail in the growth and advancement of our civilization. And so are you. But for you, it is what you do from now on that will either move our civilization forward a few tiny steps or else, ignoring much that we have already achieved, begin to march us steadily backwards.

And it is here that I begin to feel a little uncomfortable. I am an actor. I am an entertainer, and if you invite an entertainer to such an occasion, there is, it seems, an onus on that individual to be entertaining. Here is an entertainer, there is the audience, there are certain expectations. Am I right? And if those expectations are not being satisfied, then shortly I, the entertainer, will start to hear about it. Audiences often underestimate how much we, the entertainers, can hear what goes on out there. And concerning expectations, several years ago I was in a production for the Royal Shakespeare Company of *The Balcony,* by Jean Genet. I'm sure you will recall that Genet's play is a study of power, authority, and sex, set in a Paris brothel. We were performing this in the Aldwych Theatre, just around the corner from Drury Lane, and about twenty minutes into the performance one evening, we, the cast, heard quite clearly from the stalls, "Honey, are you sure this is *Phantom of the Opera?*" Oh, yes, we do know what is going on out there.

I am presently rehearsing a production of Shakespeare's *The Tempest* for the New York Shakespeare Festival, better known as Shakespeare in the Park, and some of the park old-timers have been preparing me for the somewhat unconventional audience reactions that can occur there.

It's marvelous to be rehearsing Shakespeare again. It's been ten years since I was last in a formal play of his. To be stretching oneself in the company of such a mind, for I must acknowledge that, lacking higher education in the formal sense, education informally began for me the day that I joined the Royal Shakespeare Company and continued for the next fifteen years as that man's wisdom, poetry, and vision of the world entered every corner of my life. We've only been rehearsing a few days, but already I feel the exhilaration, the challenges this playwright throws at his actors, and particularly it seems to me at the actor playing Prospero, and most dramatically in Act V, when Prospero's whole intention and objective in the play undergoes a complete transformation. You see, *The Tempest* is almost, but not quite, a revenge play. Prospero spends much of four acts using all of his intellect, energy, and magic powers to bring about the moment when his enemies, all those who have wickedly, cruelly abused him, all those who have conspired to bring about his death and that of his infant daughter, are at last in his power and at his mercy. As that moment approaches, Prospero's servant, the spirit Ariel, describes to him the pitiful state of his enemies.

Prospero asks him, "How fares the king and his followers?" And Ariel says:

> Confined together
> In the same fashion as you gave in charge,
> Just as you left them; all prisoners, sir,
> In the line-grove which weather-fends your cell;
> They cannot budge till your release. The king,
> His brother and yours, abide all three distracted
> And the remainder mourning over them,
> Brimful of sorrow and dismay; but chiefly
> Him that you term'd, sir, "The good old lord, Gonzalo;"
> His tears run down his beard, like winter's drops
> From eaves of reeds. Your charm so strongly works 'em
> That if you now beheld them, your affections
> would become tender.

And Prospero says, "Does thou think so, spirit?" Ariel says, "Mine would, sir, were I human." And Prospero replies:

> And mine shall.
> Hast thou, which art but air, a touch, a feeling
> Of their afflictions, and shall not myself,
> One of their kind, that relish all as sharply,
> Passion as they, be kindlier moved than thou art?
> Though with their high wrongs I am struck to the quick,
> Yet with my nobler reason 'gainst my fury
> Do I take part: the rarer action is
> In virtue than in vengeance.

"The rarer action is in virtue than in vengeance."

I have lived and worked in the United States for more than eight years now. This country has changed me in countless ways. It has transformed my career; it has given me material security; it made me a healthier person, and I think a nicer one. But perhaps more important than all these it has given me more fun and laughter than in all the forty-five years that have gone before. It would seem it has also changed the way I sound. After a recent interview with the BBC the journalist, with an unmistakable sneer in his voice, commented upon my "American accent." Sadly, sneers seem to be one of the commonest sounds emanating from the United Kingdom these days. Well, I certainly wasn't aware that my accent had changed, but if it has, just fine with me. If nothing else, it means that I am still open to change.

Yes, I love this country, the United States, and its people. You are admirable, optimistic, enraging, funny, and infuriating. And at times, to a European, stunningly insecure and quite, quite lost.

"The rarer action is in virtue than in vengeance."

I feel that in the United States during the last twenty years there has never been any period when that conviction needed to be articulated again and again so far as one particular issue is concerned. It is one of those fundamental issues on which future generations will judge us as a civilized, civilizing society: our respect for the sanctity of human life. Along with poverty, health, education, equal opportunity, and the environment, and the accessibility to the law for all, the existence or not of state executions will most vividly indicate the true depth of our responsibility, evolution, and compassion.

In 1976, when throughout Europe capital punishment was being voted against as an ineffective and barbarous form of punishment, the United States reinstated it, and there are presently thirty-eight states in which execution of one form or another is authorized. Thirty-eight states, including California, in which American citizens, men and women, are legally gassed, electrocuted, injected, hanged, or shot. In the last nineteen years, 272 lives have been terminated in this country by one or other of these brutal, barbaric, and grotesque means. Two hundred seventy-two occasions on which the states, in our names, have assumed an authority not simply of judges but of gods. And why? Because capital punishment is just? A life for a life? Then we should rape rapists, beat up violent husbands, castrate child molesters, and chop off the right hands of thieves. That too would be just.

Because it is a deterrent? Nationwide every set of statistics, every piece of evidence confirms that capital punishment is not a deterent. And now, in New York State, we have the incomprehensible action of a new state government reintroducing the death penalty at a time when the number of capital offenses, including murder, have during these past few years been steadily decreasing. Why? Because something stirs in him at the thought of killing? It's true that except where voters are offered alternative sentences, if this issue were put to a national referendum, the majority vote would be in favor of capital punishment. Does something stir in us too? Is there a primitive animal urge to smell blood? Maybe. But if we respond to that urge, what are we and where are we going? Not forward, that's for certain. If there is a sanctity on human life, there is a sanctity on human life. There are no clauses, no exceptions. No ifs, no buts, no special cases. Only when all human life is sacred will we begin to truly understand and truly respect its value, because then we shall also understand that we cannot hide behind our votes, behind our elected officers, and ask others, those gassers, electrocuters, injectors, and hangers to kill in our name. We demean them by employing them, and we are demeaned by their actions, and the circle of violence is perpetuated.

There are other arguments.

The innocent are wrongly executed, at least twenty-three since 1900, and forty-eight others released from death row.

The cost. The death penalty costs $90 million annually, beyond the ordinary costs of the justice system. In Texas a death penalty case costs an average of $2.3 million, about three times the cost of imprisoning in a single cell at the highest security level for forty years. On a national level these figures translate to an extra cost of a half billion dollars since 1976.

The botched executions, too many and too horrible to go into here, but without a doubt most of them would constitute an offense of being cruel and unusual punishments.

About a month ago one of your faculty, mentioning that I would be expected to make a few remarks here today, suggested that I might take into them those lines of Captain Jean-Luc Picard from the recent movie [*Star Trek*] *Generations* about how we can make a difference in the world in which we live. The next day a bomb exploded in Oklahoma City. On the following Sunday, with the country still deeply shocked by the incomprehensible horror of that act, President Clinton, leading a ceremony of national mourning, condemned the barbarism and cruelty in that taking of innocent life and vowed in the same breath that the perpetrators would be hunted down and that the maximum penalty of death would be demanded. And as I heard those words, a cry rose inside my breast. "No! Not more. Mr. President, rise above this." Somewhere the line has to be drawn, but let it not be between one death and another. The function of a leader is to lead forwards, not backwards.

I know there are many *Star Trek: The Next Generation* fans here, some who probably know the Prime Directive better than me, and though fiction I believe it is an admirable code for any society to listen to. The Federation of Planets abolished capital punishment. Gene Roddenberry's vision of the twenty-fourth century was not merely utopianism. It can be part of a blueprint for how we might live, how you might live today.

Tomorrow you will move on with an education, experience, and with *choices*. Make a difference.

My thanks to you for inviting Wendy and me to share this day with you. Congratulations and good luck.

Hank Aaron

Emory University School of Law
May 2, 1995

A model athlete as well as an eloquent and courageous
advocate for civil rights, Hank Aaron is a true champion. In
1974 he broke Babe Ruth's career home-run mark, going on to
a record 757 career home-runs over a twenty-two-year, Hall of
Fame career in major league baseball. Here he talks to Emory
Law School's Class of 1995 about having the courage to
succeed.

Let me congratulate each of you students for a great accomplishment, earning your law degree from one of the finest universities in the land. And thank you for letting me share in this achievement, first by honoring me with a Doctor of Laws degree and also by inviting me to speak on this special occasion.

It seems to me that the members of this class are starting your law careers at an unusual time in the legal profession. Never before have lawyers been so prominent in the public eye. They're constantly in the news with every word they say and every maneuver they make, scrutinized and analyzed in the smallest detail.

Watching all this coverage of famous attorneys, you students might feel a bit like I did the first time I watched big-league hitters up close. I remember having two reactions.

First, that given the chance, I could hit big-league pitching too. Second, that the difference between a .300 and a .280 hitter was pretty obvious. It boiled down to what the hitter did when he got *his* pitch,* the one type of pitch he was looking for and wanting to swing at. A .300 hitter would hit his pitch every time, but as often as not, when a .280 hitter would get his pitch, he'd foul it off.

The same difference seems to be true of most of what we attempt in life. Playing ball or practicing law, a person gets just an occasional opportunity to do something great. To come through in a big way. When the time comes, just two things matter. How well prepared we are to seize the moment. And having the courage to take our best swing.

As a graduate of Emory Law School, you start off about as well prepared as a young lawyer can be. Because this is a great school with an outstanding reputation. Through the years Emory law graduates have gone on to change their communities for the better and to bring honor to the profession. People will expect a lot from you because of where you come from.

And don't ever be afraid of high expectations. A great heritage is something we can't escape, even if we want to. It's like a foundation under our feet, we didn't put it there, but we're standing on it anyway. And either we build on the foundation, or it will crumble away underneath us.

In the mid-1950s, when I was getting established in major league baseball, black players were building on the heritage created by Jackie Robinson, a heritage of professional excellence and personal dignity. All of us were conscious of living up to Jackie's heritage. In how he played the game and how he treated the pressures of being treated differently, as we nearly always were back then.

But only in later years would I come to realize how re-

---

*Though Aaron could hit a hanging curve, or any other pitch, out of the park on any given day, Aaron's pitch was a fastball, low and in. Cardinals pitcher Curt Simmons once remarked, "Throwing a fastball by Hank Aaron is like trying to sneak the sun past a rooster."

markable the Jackie Robinson legacy really was. The truth
dawned in 1973 and 1974, as I was getting closer to the all-
time home-run record held by the greatest white hero in the
history of the game. I have to tell you, I knew there would
be some racial venom . . . but the extent of it shocked me.
There were threats made on me and to my family.

At the same time I had a lot of support from my teammates. From other ballplayers, white and black, from family
and friends. From many fans and from media people who had
long ago rejected the notion that a ballplayer's color mattered
in the least.

Which made Jackie Robinson's achievements of twenty-
five years earlier all the more remarkable. He had very little
support. He was surrounded by active hostility even from
some of his teammates. But Jackie knew he was getting his
pitch. And he nailed it like few ballplayers have ever done,
before or since. Not just for himself. But for me, for Mays,
for McCovey, Clemente, Stargell, David Justice, Barry
Bonds, Ken Griffey . . . for every single black player in the
game today. And even more importantly, for millions of
American kids, black and white, who today would think of
segregated sports as the most bizarre idea in the world.

What you and I do when we get our pitch makes a tremendous difference, even to people we'll never know. As a
lawyer you'll have more opportunities to hit your pitch than
most people do. That's just the nature of the job. No matter
what kind of law you practice, in the courtroom, in government, in a corporation, in a public interest law firm, you'll
be on the front line, shaping society.

You can be sure your pitch is going to come. It's all in
what you do with it. God has given you the talent to handle
it. Emory has given you the preparation.

Reach down inside yourself, and you'll find the courage.
The courage to risk something great when the great opportunity presents itself. Good luck, and God bless each of you.

Ross Perot

Boston University
May 22, 1994

H. Ross Perot, one of America's wealthiest men, formed
Electronic Data Systems in 1962 with $1,000 of his savings.
He sold the company to General Motors in 1984 for a
staggering $2.5 billion. As an independent candidate for
President in 1992 Perot won 19 percent of the popular vote, the
best showing for a third-party candidate since Teddy Roosevelt
ran for the Bull Moose party in 1912. In 1993 Perot formed
the political watchdog group United We Stand. In 1995 he
formed the Reform party and ran as its presidential candidate
in 1996.

It's great to be with you on your graduation day! You are
the Class of 1994. You and others like you will, to a large
extent, determine what the twenty-first century is going to be
like. Are you going to make it the best in this great country's
history? There we go! There must be somebody out there in
television land, you know, huddled up in a dark room saying,
"Oo, it's going to be so hard."

The challenges we face are nothing. You are in a historic
spot. You are near Plymouth Rock. You are where the Boston Tea Party took place. We're talking about high-risk ven-
tures here. You are near Bunker Hill. You are in the state
where the Kennedy family lived. I don't have to tell you the
sacrifices that John F. Kennedy, Robert Kennedy, and Mrs.
Kennedy made for this great country. What we're talking
about in rebuilding for the twenty-first century is a piece of

cake compared to giving your life. Can we agree on that? Okay.

We are the luckiest group of people in the world. Angela from Iowa cannot come to Boston University, and she surely can't go find a pyramid in the middle of nowhere that a bunch of Ph.D.'s couldn't find for decades, right? Dr. Brown grew up in an orphanage, wanted to be a surgeon, forget it.* Michael didn't forget it. You say, look at the obstacles she had to overcome. Her challenge was like climbing a cliff barehanded covered with ice. She did it. That's what America is all about.

I'll tell you one more example. I'll never come to Boston without bringing up the name John Connors because he is just a little bit older than you. He grew up in this area. Great family. He went to Worcester Polytechnic. He was a chemical engineer. He went to Heidelberg in his junior year, didn't know how to speak German, and got honors grades in chemistry. Now all you folks at the top of the pile will admit, that's a pretty tough challenge: learn a language and get honors grades. Then he came out, and I think of John when I look at all you guys out there in the uniform here with the faculty. John was a naval officer. John was a Navy SEAL. John was in Bethesda Hospital when Panama went down. John had the perfect ticket not to go. John went AWOL to be with his men. John's mission was to take Noriega at the [Panama City] airport. That's a pretty central mission in that effort. Noriega never came to the airport. John Connors gave his life. Surely you can understand why I cannot come to Boston and not mention his name. He's a man we must always honor.

I wanted to congratulate you, and now I'd like to thank

*Michael S. Brown. Dr. Brown is currently professor of molecular genetics at the University of Texas Southwestern Medical School.

the faculty. With your great talents you could have pursued many and more financially rewarding careers, but you chose to dedicate your lives to molding tomorrow's leaders. And there are a lot of ways to make more money than doing that. But they have given themselves and given their lives to you. They, the faculty, will make a huge difference in determining what our country will be twenty and thirty years from now because of the training you received. What they have done is far more important than what they could have done to make a lot of money. People who give their lives in service should always be recognized. I ask every person here who is graduating to seek out those professors that made a big difference in your lives and thank them today and give them a big hug.

Just as important, there's a group out there that I just love, and those are the folks in the orange vests. And I finally asked Dr. Silber, "Who are the people in the orange vests?" He says, "These are people who work all across the campus." These are the people who—we used to call them housemothers in the dormitories—these are the people who keep the place going. They're out here today to participate in your graduation, and guess what? They're not being paid. They are giving their time so that your graduation will be perfect. Make sure you thank them because if they hadn't been here all four years when you were here when the heat went off in the middle of winter, you'd have missed them, right? Don't ever forget. They're vitally important to this place.

I'd like to talk to the graduates whose parents are here today that had to work and sacrifice so that you could get your degree. In the euphoria of this day, please sit down, let them know how much you appreciate their sacrifices. And let them know how much you love them because they have really gone to the wall so you could have this great opportunity. Don't just take it for granted. They paid for it. Thank them for it. But now that's small stuff. Talk is cheap, right? Here's the way you thank them for it. Go out and spend the rest of your life showing them they made a good investment, fair enough? Okay.

Now I'd like to talk to the graduates who were the first in their families to ever attend college. This is the American Dream—have we got some? Okay, terrific! The dream lives. I had that experience. My father had to drop out of school and work as a Texas cowboy, didn't finish high school—far smarter than I am. My mother got to finish high school but couldn't afford to go to college. They worked and sacrificed all their lives so that my sister and I could have the dream they never had. Your parents have that same dream for you, and they have worked and sacrificed. Please remember that through you they are realizing the dream they had that never materialized. Please understand how important your graduation is to them. Thank them, let them know how much you love them, and hug them hard. You have a special obligation to do something important with the chance they never had. If you do, their sacrifices for you will have all been worthwhile, and I know you will.

I propose, I know you'll do that individually, but for all these different groups I've just mentioned, I propose that we take just a minute and take advantage of an old British custom. It's called three cheers, and the way you do it is, I say, "Hip, hip," and you say, "Hooray," three times, and I hope, you know, at this level you can, you know, pick that up in a hurry. So what I would like to do is to propose three cheers to the parents, to the faculty, to all these great people who are here today who work behind the scenes to make this great university go . . . so I propose three cheers to them. Hip, hip, hooray. Okay, let's warm it up. Hip, hip, hooray. Hip, hip, hooray. Hip, hip, hooray. God bless you all.

All right, now let's get down to you. Let me talk to the

best and the brightest. Let me talk to the ones who finished at the top. That must be all of you. Okay, I'm worried about you. Don't be cocky. Don't be arrogant; be humble. My big concern based on years of dealing with the best and brightest kids that at many times it's so easy for them that many times they never achieve their full potential. Make sure you do. Get up every morning and say, "This wonderful mind that I have is a genetic gift. I'm lucky to have it. I'm not going to be cocky and arrogant about it. I'm going to use it to its full potential."

You have something like a perfectly large stereo system that has no static. It's a gift. You can read complex, scientific literature once, remember it, make a perfect score. Most of us have a lot of static in our heads and can't do that. Your minds can go places that our minds can never go, and you can do things that our minds will never let us do. And the minus to that is that success breeds arrogance and complacency. I've worked with thousands of young people over the years, and guess what? The average people always beat the best and the brightest. It's one of my frustrations.

Since you have this gift, make sure you use it to the outer edges of its capabilities, and then you will make a huge difference. So far I am concerned that success has been too easy for you, even though I'm sure right now you don't think it has. You have not had to sweat intellectually, and let me describe that. You don't know what it is not to finish first. You don't know what it is to strive and fail, pick yourself up, dust yourself off, and try again. You don't know what it is to finish the race and not get the gold medal. The people who have had to do that again and again build a big advantage over you. They're used to disappointments. They're used to recovering from defeat. They've learned to persevere. I challenge you to use it all and achieve your full potential.

Now I'd like to talk to another group, the group that had to struggle to graduate. I don't worry a bit about you because adversity breeds strength. You're going to do just fine. Some of you had to read the same lesson five times, then you had to underline it, then you had to outline it, and finally, in order just to pass the course, you had to memorize it. On top of that you probably had to seek help from your friends and professor, and you say, "Gee, Ross, how do you know all that?" Well, I fell into that category. I remember that very clearly. Don't think you're dumb. You've built in a big advantage. You've learned a priceless lesson. You've learned to persevere. You don't quit. You don't give up. You expect life to be hard, and when it's hard, you walk around grinning because that's just the way it is. You know you have to pay an extra price to get there, and you pay it.

I've had the good fortune to meet many people in life that you would consider successful. In nearly every case, guess what, they have average intellects. It gives them an advantage because they understand they have to surround themselves with very talented people, and they get the multiplier effect. And again, the people who have been most successful have failed again and again. You never see their failures and disappointments, but they're all there. And they are the foundation upon which their huge successes rest. But one of the things they learned as young people was don't get discouraged and don't give up.

To the best and brightest again, just remember to keep it in perspective. Somewhere on the streets of India right now a person brighter than you is starving to death. You're the luckiest person in the world because you happen to be here. Somebody better and brighter than you is coming out of Vietnam on a boat, will probably drown at sea, and never had the opportunities that you and I have had. Even more relevant, across this country there are people working third shift just getting by in factories that are smarter than you and I.

You say, "Oh, come on, Ross." Don Efland, a young man that went to work at General Motors factories, he was so bright he was accepted at MIT and couldn't afford to go. Then he was so bright he was accepted at West Point and failed an eye exam and spent his life on the factory floor. He was the first factory worker to ever speak to the board [of directors]. His speech was brilliant. I asked him if I could read it at some later date as my own just to see the audience reaction. He laughed and said yes. I did it one night at the United Nations to a who's who of corporate America and got a standing ovation. When I told them whose speech it was, if I could have filmed their faces, I could have retired just selling that film. Now there is justice in life. Don Efland is now retired and guess what he does? He lectures at MIT, the school he couldn't afford to attend. Now that's an opportunity that would only come in America.

See, Don didn't get the breaks. You say, "What's the point in telling that story?" Don didn't get the breaks you have. The ball bounced the right way in your life—makes a tremendous difference. If you'll go through life feeling lucky, with a big dose of humility rather than feeling special, you'll beat those cocky guys and girls ten times out often. When you see people in distress, because you've been so fortunate, never look down on them. Just say, "There but by the grace of God go I," and help them. Now that's what makes America work. You say, "Well, can't we get a government program for them?" Yeah, but it'll be tenth-rate compared to you helping them right on the spot.

Be a giver, not a taker. We're coming out of the me generation. I hope as you come into the world out of school, we're going into the we generation because if people are self-ish, society doesn't work. All through life, just ask yourself, "Does it work?" No, selfishness doesn't work. It's as old as the history of man. Our generation, in the me generation, has dug a deep hole for you to fill and you say, "Gee, are we going to have to fill it?" The answer is yes, and you say, "Why?" Because it's there. We'll all have to get busy and fill it together. You need to be a giver, not a taker. Help other people at all times. Do a good turn daily. You learn that in Scouting as a child. It works. It makes society work. Are you going to spend your life looking after number one or are you going to create opportunities for other people? If you can ever cross that bridge, that's your ticket to financial success. Create opportunities for other people. The story of my business career. I surrounded myself with people who are a lot better and brighter than I am. I listened to their ideas, we took their ideas, and they carried me on my shoulders from victory, to victory, to victory. Pretty simple stuff. One person can't get much done. A lot of people can get a lot done.

Now anytime I'm with a group like you, they always say, "Now, Ross, we want to be successful." Well, okay, we'll talk about that, but what is success? You say, "Well, success is making a lot of money." I say no, you're on the wrong track. Success is being the best at whatever you do. You say, "Can I just be the best in my hometown?" No. "Can I be the best in my country?" No. You've got to be the best in the world because we live in a tiny world. You say, "Well, can I go for the red ribbon?" No, there's no red ribbon for second place in business. You either win or lose. You've got to be the best. "Now," you say, "we're talking business." No, if you're going to be a minister, be the finest. If you're going to be a doctor, teacher, or social worker, be the finest. I hope you can't sleep at night unless you're achieving your full potential because that determines what our country will be.

Now let's look at how things really happen as opposed to how many of you think they happen. For example, the Wright brothers just had to fly. You say, "Okay, that's fine, but the Wright brothers were two bicycle repairmen." Like Angela from Iowa, right? She can't find a pyramid. They can't fly. There was a Dr. Langley that had government grants when today's world would say, "Oh, well, just shut down the Wright brothers." Right? No, they had to fly and they, every time you see . . . look up there, look at those trails going across the sky. Two bicycle repairmen from Dayton, Ohio, did that. That's the magic of America, but they had to do it, and they got it done. Thomas Edison's teachers thought he was dumb. Don't forget, Dr. Brown, some of her teachers thought she was trouble. When I find a character like that, I get excited because inevitably those are highly creative, talented people. Every time you land at night, look down on the city, look at all those lights and say, "A dumb guy, Thomas Edison, did all that." He had to do it if you study his life.

You say, "Ross, those are old examples." Fine, let's come up to modern times. A young man so bright they let him sit in engineering schools at Stanford when he was in high school, but so poor he could not attend, was in his father's garage playing with integrated circuits, and his dad walked in one day and said, "Son, make something you can sell or get a job." And sixty days later the first Apple computer in a wooden box was sold, and the computer industry was revolutionized by a high school graduate. You're saying, "Is there still opportunity in America?" Oh, boy, is there opportunity in America! When a high school graduate can take on and beat IBM. You say, "Is that the only one?" No. How about Bill Gates, Microsoft—dropped out of Harvard. The rest is history.

You say, "I really want to make a lot of money, Ross." I'd say, well, that's the worst way in the world to go about it. If you have that as your goal, you probably won't make it, and if you get it, you probably won't be happy after you've got it. Just have being the best at what you are, build a great team, the other comes as a byproduct.

Financial success and happiness are unrelated. I've had the interesting opportunity to know most of the people that you would think of as the wealthiest people in the world. A huge number of them are very unhappy. I am no happier today than I was as a boy in the Depression in Texarcana. I was rich then because of my parents, and my riches now are Margot [Perot] and five wonderful children. And you say, "But, Ross, isn't the money . . . ?" No, after you make it, about all you can do is give it away to good causes, and interestingly enough you've got to be careful it doesn't ruin your children, and God bless Margot, we've got five out of five that it didn't ruin. And there's a final story here: It's harder to give it away intelligently than it is to make it. So it's kinda interesting.

Everybody asks me, "How do I find a good job, Ross?" It's tough to find a good job today. I say, okay, that's exciting, that means they don't just come to you. That means you have to go out and look. Now at the top of the pile, from our best and brightest and finest lead schools you mean they're not sending teams to interview me? I said, thank goodness, no, not this year. You've got to go out there and knock on doors. This is going to make you smart, street smart and tough. You're going to find the right job. "How do I find the right job?" You don't quite know what you want to be yet, but if you go out and talk and interview and interview and interview, you'll find something you have to do, then just do it. Then let's assume you misfired. Go back and do it again. You'll find the right opportunity for yourself. It's an inexact science.

I've had people say, "You mean, I should travel on my ticket?" Absolutely. If it's a bus ticket, go to where you want to go, interview that company, get in line, and the rest will be history. Play to your strengths. Everybody thinks they need to be a business executive. Well, thank goodness the Wright brothers didn't want to be one. Thank goodness Dr. De Bakey, the famous heart surgeon, didn't want to be one. Thank goodness Dr. Brown didn't want to be a business executive. Thank goodness Mother Teresa didn't want to be a business executive. Don't get carried away with the executive thing. Just play your strengths and do what fits. You say, "But everybody else is doing it." That's the best reason in the world not to go with the herd. Follow your instincts. Listen to your own drumming.

If you are going to have other people work for you, let me just take a minute and go through what you've got to do. You've got to develop the skills, their skills, you've got to motivate them, and you've got to tap their full potential. You manage inventories; you don't manage people. You lead and inspire people. Interestingly enough, leadership's not taught in many colleges. You've got to earn the trust and respect of others every day. You've got to be candid. You've got to be honest. You've got to live in the center of the field of ethical behavior. And treat others like you would want to be treated, and everybody's sitting there, saying, "Well, wait a minute, that's the Golden Rule." That's right, it's worked for two thousand years. It's in just about every religion you hear about. You say, "Wait a minute, I don't have to do that. I'm the boss," but that young person reporting to you is a human being, and there's something inside the least significant human being in the world, if there is such a thing, that says, "I am unique, I am special, there's only one person in the world like me. Treat me as a human being, and if you do, the success of your team will go through the roof."

Don't force everyone to conform to your ideas. My business success rests squarely on the ideas of young, very young, very inexperienced engineers who were very inarticulate who would come into my office [cheers]. There you go. I'm assuming you're cheering about young engineers, not inarticulate, but that's okay. But mine were inarticulate. They would come in and mumble in computerese some idea that only because I understood the industry I could grasp. We would take their idea, and the rest was history. Always the really incredible ideas came from the young people.

Listen, listen, listen to the people that do the work, and when you compete, keep in mind my little company had to compete against IBM. We were the Bad News Bears; they were the New York Yankees. Never forget, young people, when you go out here with no money in your pocket, brains and wits will beat money ten times out of ten. Beat 'em with brains and wits. We started from nowhere. Margot loaned me a thousand dollars, and we beat and we beat and we beat, and finally we got to the biggest procurement in the history of the industry. When the dust clears, it was the Bad News Bears. My company and IBM, it was going to be a two-year war. They had unlimited resources; we didn't have much. They assigned 350 people to the competition; we assigned 15. What's the story? Small, high-talent team will beat an army anytime. To make a long story short, I was with the team the night they won. They were all excited. They traded thousands of jobs.

But now the one thing I've left out is this: that in the middle of the competition the team is discouraged, and our great president, whose grandfather had to flee Russia, the American Dream, two generations ago lived in an attic in

Brooklyn as a tailor. His grandson is the president of EDS, walked into the room, and our fifteen men said, "We can't win, but it'll be a great experience." And Mort* didn't chew anybody out. He just walked up quietly to the front row and wrote down the seven criteria by which we'd be judged, and then he said, "You guys are missing the point; we'll beat them seven to zero," and he walked out.

From that point on, that was the crusade. I was with them the night they won. They were thrilled they had won. They were thrilled they had created thousands of jobs. They were thrilled with the bonuses and raises and so on and so forth. But the thing that meant more than anything else was that they beat the rest of the world seven to zero. Now that's what you've gotta play for. Play to win every point.

You've got such an opportunity in your life. There's so much you can do, and I have to talk to you for one minute. The most important thing you're going to do is choose your husband and wife. Take your time, it's fun to look, but do it right. And when you marry, remember you swear at the church to stay together for life. Your children need you, and I can tell you with no question that you will judge yourself by how your children turn out. It takes both of you to rear those little children. Forget everything I've talked about so far. In terms of importance this is the most important thing I can say about you. Really make sure you make that decision correctly. Really give yourself to your children just as your parents gave themselves to you because they are the future of your generation.

And finally, live life to the fullest. Get up every morning grinning. Don't be a talker; be a doer. Remember Lech Walesa's words to our Congress when he said, "Words are plen-

---

*Morton H. Meyerson. Former president of Electronic Data Systems, currently employed by Perot Systems.

tiful, but deeds are precious. Be a doer of deeds." See, in our country, if we have potholes in the street, we have a press conference on potholes. Be a person who gets hot asphalt, a shovel and fills the potholes, skips the press conference. That's what our country dies for. Don't worry about how things look; focus on how things are and what needs to be done. When you foul up, just take responsibility for your mistakes. Mistakes, if they're honest, are like skinned knees. They're painful; they heal in a hurry; they're learning experiences. You can't have a successful life sitting in the sideline. Whining won't change things.

Teddy Roosevelt summed it up, and in closing I'll read his words. "It's not the critic who counts. It's not the man who points out the strong man stumbled or where the doer of deeds could have done them better. The credit belongs to the man in the arena whose face is marred by dust and sweat and blood who strives valiantly, who errs and comes short again and again, who knows the great enthusiasms, the great devotions, who spends himself in a worthy cause, who at best, in the end, knows the triumph of high achievement and who, at worst, if he fails at least fails while daring greatly." What I'm really saying, I would rather see you dare greatly and fail than not dare. Because everything you do involves risk and you learn from your failures. I know you'll be good citizens and parents. I know you'll be givers and not takers. I know you will spend your lives in the arena.

As soon as this ceremony is over, find your professors, find your parents, find the folks in the orange vests. Thank them; hug them; let them know how much you appreciate what they've done. Every morning just wake up grinning, no matter how tough things are. Say, "I'm going to make today better than yesterday no matter how tough yesterday was." Don't ever get discouraged. Live Churchill's shortest speech. Here's the whole speech: "Never give in, never give in,

never, never, never." Live that speech, and finally, and I am
closing now, just live this—live this, and you'll have a great
life. A bell is no bell till you ring it. Don't just sit there and
look at a bell; ring it. A song is no song till you sing it.
Forget everything I've said so far, and listen to these last two
lines. This is the most important thing I'll say: Love in your
heart isn't put there to stay; love isn't love till you give it
away. Just spend your life giving it away, and you'll get it
back.

V

A Look Back

In the final analysis, our most basic common link is that we all inhabit this small planet. We all breathe the same air. We all cherish our children's future. And we are all mortal....

—JOHN F. KENNEDY

Ralph Waldo Emerson

Harvard Divinity School
July 15, 1838

*One of the leading essayists of the nineteenth century, Ralph
Waldo Emerson, along with other transcendentalists, such as
Henry David Thoreau, Margaret Fuller, and Theodore Parker,
emphasized individualism, self-examination, and the beauty of
nature and of the creative process. This address to the senior
class at the Divinity School of Harvard University attracted
such controversy that the university refused to invite Emerson,
a Harvard graduate, back for any school events for thirty
years. An excerpt follows.*

. . . Jesus Christ belonged to the true race of prophets. He
saw with open eye the mystery of the soul. Drawn by its
severe harmony, ravished with its beauty, he lived in it, and
had his being there. Alone in all history, he estimated the
greatness of man. One man was true to what is in you and
me. He saw that God incarnates himself in man, and evermore
goes forth anew to take possession of his world. He said, in
this jubilee of sublime emotion, "I am divine. Through me,
God acts; through me, speaks. Would you see God, see me;
or, see thee, when thou also thinkest as I now think." But
what a distortion did his doctrine and memory suffer in the
same, in the next, and the following ages! There is no doctrine of the Reason which will bear to be taught by the Understanding. The understanding caught this high chant from
the poet's lips, and said, in the next age, "This was Jehovah
come down out of heaven. I will kill you, if you say he was

a man." The idioms of his language, and the figures of his rhetoric, have usurped the place of his truth; and churches are not built on his principles, but on his tropes. Christianity became a Mythus, as the poetic teaching of Greece and of Egypt, before. He spoke of miracles; for he felt that man's life was a miracle, and all that man doth, and he knew that this daily miracle shines, as the character ascends. But the word Miracle, as pronounced by Christian churches, gives a false impression; it is Monster. It is not one with the blowing clover and the falling rain.

He felt respect for Moses and the prophets; but no unfit tenderness at postponing their initial revelations, to the hour and the man that now is; to the eternal revelation in the heart. Thus was he a true man. Having seen that the law in us is commanding, he would not suffer it to be commanded. Boldly, with hand, and heart, and life, he declared it was God. Thus is he, as I think, the only soul in history who has appreciated the worth of a man.

1. In this point of view we become very sensible of the first defect of historical Christianity. Historical Christianity has fallen into the error that corrupts all attempts to communicate religion. As it appears to us, and as it has appeared for ages, it is not the doctrine of the soul, but an exaggeration of the personal, the positive, the ritual. It has dwelt, it dwells, with noxious exaggeration about the *person* of Jesus. The soul knows no persons. It invites every man to expand to the full circle of the universe, and will have no preferences but those of spontaneous love. But by this eastern monarchy of a Christianity, which indolence and fear have built, the friend of man is made the injurer of man. The manner in which his name is surrounded with expressions, which were once sallies of admiration and love, but are now petrified into official titles, kills all generous sympathy and liking. All who hear me, feel, that the language that describes Christ to Europe and Amer-

ica, is not the style of friendship and enthusiasm to a good and noble heart, but is appropriated and formal—paints a demigod, as the Orientals or the Greeks would describe Osiris or Apollo. Accept the injurious impositions of our early cat-echetical instruction, and even honesty and self-denial were but splendid sins, if they did not wear the Christian name. One would rather be "A pagan, suckled in a creed outworn," than to be defrauded of his manly right in coming into nature, and finding not names and places, not land and professions, but even virtue and truth foreclosed and monopolized. You shall not be a man even. You shall not own the world, you shall not dare, and live after the infinite Law that is in you, and in company with the infinite Beauty which heaven and earth reflect to you in all lovely forms; but you must sub-ordinate your nature to Christ's nature; you must accept our interpretations; and take his portrait as the vulgar draw it.

That is always best which gives me to myself. The sublime is excited in me by the great stoical doctrine, Obey thyself. That which shows God in me, fortifies me. That which shows God out of me, makes me a wart and a wen. There is no longer a necessary reason for my being. Already the long shadows of untimely oblivion creep over me, and I shall de-cease forever.

The divine bards are the friends of my virtue, of my in-tellect of my strength. They admonish me, that the gleams which flash across my mind, are not mine, but God's; that they had the like, and were not disobedient to the heavenly vision. So I love them. Noble provocations go out from them, inviting me to resist evil; to subdue the world; and to Be. And thus by his holy thoughts, Jesus serves us, and thus only. To aim to convert a man by miracles, is a profanation of the soul. A true conversion, a true Christ, is now, as always, to be made, by the reception of beautiful sentiments. It is true that a great and rich soul, like his, falling among the simple, does so preponderate, that, as his did, it names the world. The world seems to them to exist for him, and they have not yet drunk so deeply of his sense, as to see that only by coming again to themselves, or to God in themselves, can they grow forevermore. It is a low benefit to give me something; it is a high benefit to enable me to do somewhat of myself. The time is coming when all men will see, that the gift of God to the soul is not a vaunting, overpowering, excluding sanctity, but a sweet, natural goodness, a goodness like thine and mine, and that so invites thine and mine to be and to grow.

The injustice of the vulgar tone of preaching is not less flagrant to Jesus, than to the souls which it profanes. The preachers do not see that they make his gospel not glad, and shear him of the locks of beauty and the attributes of heaven. When I see a majestic Epaminondas, or Washington; when I see among my contemporaries, a true orator, an upright judge, a dear friend; when I vibrate to the melody and fancy of a poem; I see beauty that is to be desired. And so lovely, and with yet more entire consent of my human being, sounds in my ear the severe music of the bards that have sung of the true God in all ages. Now do not degrade the life and dialogues of Christ out of the circle of this charm, by insulation and peculiarity. Let them lie as they befell, alive and warm, part of human life, and of the landscape, and of the cheerful day.

2. The second defect of the traditionary and limited way of using the mind of Christ is a consequence of the first; this, namely; that the Moral Nature, that Law of laws, whose revelations introduce greatness,—yea, God himself, into the open soul, is not explored as the fountain of the established teaching in society. Men have come to speak of the revelation as somewhat long ago given and done, as if God were dead. The injury to faith throttles the preacher; and the goodliest of institutions becomes an uncertain and inarticulate voice.

It is very certain that it is the effect of conversation with the beauty of the soul, to beget a desire and need to impart to others the same knowledge and love. If utterance is denied, the thought lies like a burden on the man. Always the seer is a sayer. Somehow his dream is told: somehow he publishes it with solemn joy: sometimes with pencil on canvas; sometimes with chisel on stone; sometimes in towers and aisles of granite, his soul's worship is builded; sometimes in anthems of indefinite music; but clearest and most permanent, in words.

The man enamored of this excellency, becomes its priest or poet. The office is coeval with the world. But observe the condition, the spiritual limitation of the office. The spirit only can teach. Not any profane man, not any sensual, not any liar, not any slave can teach, but only he can give, who has; he only can create, who is. The man on whom the soul descends, through whom the soul speaks, alone can teach. Courage, piety, love, wisdom, can teach; and every man can open his door to these angels, and they shall bring him the gift of tongues. But the man who aims to speak as books enable, as synods use, as the fashion guides, and as interest commands, babbles. Let him hush.

To this holy office, you propose to devote yourselves. I wish you may feel your call in throbs of desire and hope. The office is the first in the world. It is of that reality, that it cannot suffer the deduction of any falsehood. And it is my duty to say to you, that the need was never greater of new revelation than now. From the views I have already expressed, you will infer the sad conviction, which I share, I believe, with numbers, of the universal decay and now almost death of faith in society. The soul is not preached. The Church seems to totter to its fall, almost all life extinct. On this occasion, any complaisance would be criminal, which told you, whose hope and commission it is to preach the faith of Christ, that the faith of Christ is preached. . . .

W. E. B. Du Bois

Fisk University
June 15, 1898

William Edward Burghardt Du Bois was the first African American to receive a doctorate from Harvard (in 1895). He wrote numerous books and essays and helped found the National Association for the Advancement of Colored People (NAACP) in 1910. A graduate of Fisk University in 1888, Du Bois returned ten years later to deliver this address. Although he discusses the various professions African Americans should pursue, the speech is most remarkable for his discussion of the anxiety many college students felt about entering the work force, a theme still common in commencement addresses a century later. The following is a small excerpt from his address.

To the young ears that harken behind college walls at the confused murmur of the world beyond, there comes at times a strangely discordant note to mar the music of their lives. Men tell them that college is a play world—the mirage of real life; the place where men climb or seek to climb heights whence they must sooner or later sink into the dust of real life. Scarcely a commencement season passes but what, amid congratulation and rejoicing, amid high resolve and lofty sentiment, stalks this pale, half-mocking ghost, crying to the newborn bachelor in arts. You have played—now comes work.

And, therefore, students of the class of '98, I have thought to take this oft-repeated idea and talk with you in this last hour of your college days about the relation to which, in your lives, a liberal education bears to bread-winning.

And first, young men and women, I heartily join in congratulating you to who has been vouchsafed the vision splendid—you who stand where I once stood,

> When meadow, grove, and stream,
>   The earth, and every common sight,
> To me did seem
>   Apparelled in celestial light
> The glory and the freshness of a dream.

And yet not a dream, but a mighty reality—a glimpse of the higher life, the broader possibilities of humanity, which is granted to the man who, amid the rush and roar of living, pauses four short years to learn what living means.

The vision of the rich meaning of life, which comes to you as students, as men of culture, comes dimly not at all to the plodding masses of men, and even to men of the high estate it comes too often blurred and distorted by selfishness and greed. But you have seen it in the freshness and sunshine of youth: here you have talked with Aristotle and Shakespeare, have learned of Euclid, have heard the solemn drama of a world, and thought the thoughts of seers and heroes of the world that was. Out of such lore, out of such light and shade, has the vision of the world appeared before you: you have not all comprehended it; you have, many of you, but glanced at its brilliant hues, and have missed the speaking splendor of the background.

I remember how once I stood near the ancient cathedral at Berne, looking at the Alps; I heard the rushing waters below and knew their music; I saw the rolling fields beyond and thought them pretty; then I saw the hills and the towering masses of dark mountains; they were beautiful, and yet I saw them with a tinge of disappointment, but even as I turned away, I glanced toward the sky, and then my heart leaped—for there above the meadows and the waters, above the hills and the mountains, blazed in the evening sunshine, the mighty, snow-clad peaks of the high Alps, glistening and glorious with the hues of the rainbow, in spotless purity and awful majesty. And so many a man to whom opportunity has unveiled some revelation of the broader, truer world, has turned away from it, half seen and half known.

But some have seen the vision, have comprehended all the meaning of a liberal education; and now, as you turn away, half-regretfully, half-gladly, what relation has this day of transfiguration to the hard, cold paths of the world beyond these walls? Is it to be but a memory and a longing, or if more than this, how much more?

I presume that few of you have fully realized that with tomorrow morning you begin to earn your own bread and butter; that today is the commencement of a new life on which you are to find self-support by daily toil. And I am glad if you have not given this matter too much thought or worry, for, surely, if you have done well your college work you have had other things to think of, problems of life and humanity far broader than your own single destiny; not that you have neglected dreams and plans of parts that you might play in life, but that you have scarce thought out its dry details. And, therefore, to most of you, the nearness of real life dawned this morning with a certain suddenness; with something of that dark dismay with which the human creator faces his own creature. . . .

. . . It is now ten years since I stood amid these walls on my commencement morning, ten years full of toil and happiness and sorrow, and the full delight of hard work. And as I look back on that youthful gleam, and see the vision splendid, the trailing clouds of glory that lighted then the wide array of life, I am ever glad that I stepped into the world guided by strong faith in its promises, and inspired by no sordid aims. And from that world I come back to welcome you, my brothers and sisters. I cannot promise you happiness always, but I can promise you divine discontent with the imperfect. I cannot promise you success—'tis not in the mortals to command success.

But as you step into life I can give you three watchwords: first, you are Negroes, members of that dark, historic race that from the world's dawn has slept to hear the trumpet sermons sound through our ears. Cherish unwavering faith in the blood of your fathers, and make sure this last triumph of humanity. Remember next, that you are gentlemen and ladies, trained in the liberal arts and subjects in that vast kingdom of culture that has lighted the world from its infancy and guided it through bigotry and falsehood and sin. As such, let us see in you an unfaltering honesty wedded to that finer courtesy and breeding which is the heritage of the well-trained and well-born. And, finally, remember that you are the sons of Fisk University, that venerable mother who rose out of the blood and dust of battle to work the triumphs of the Prince of Peace. The mighty blessing of all her sons and daughters encompass you, and the sad sacrifice of every pure soul, living and dead, that has made her what she is, bend its dark wings about you and make you brave and good! And then, through the weary striving and disappointment of life, fear not for the end, even though you fail:

> Truth forever on the scaffold
>   Wrong forever on the throne
> Yet that scaffold sways in the future,
>   And behind the dim unknown
> Standeth God with the shadow,
>   Keeping watch above his own.

George C. Marshall

Harvard University
June 5, 1947

Secretary of State George Marshall's commencement address at Harvard in 1947 ranks with Churchill's Iron Curtain address as one of the most important speeches of the post–World War II era. As Army chief of staff during the war, General Marshall knew all too well how the war had devastated Europe, and he sought to rebuild Western Europe through a massive American economic and humanitarian aid program. In this address he outlined this program, commonly known as the Marshall Plan. He won the Nobel Prize in 1953 for his efforts. Here is the speech in its entirety.

I need not tell you, gentlemen, that the world situation is very serious. That must be apparent to all intelligent people. I think one difficulty is that the problem is one of such enormous complexity that the very mass of facts presented to the public by press and radio make it exceedingly difficult for the man in the street to reach a clear appraisement of the situation. Furthermore, the people of this country are distant from the troubled areas of the earth and it is hard for them to comprehend the plight and consequent reactions of the long-suffering peoples, and the effect of those reactions on their governments in connection with our efforts to promote peace in the world.

In considering the requirements for the rehabilitation of Europe, the physical loss of life, the visible destruction of cities, factories, mines and railroads was correctly estimated but it has become obvious during recent months that this visible destruction was probably less serious than the dislocation of the entire fabric of European economy. For the past ten years conditions have been highly abnormal. The feverish preparation for war and the more feverish maintenance of the war effort engulfed all aspects of national economies. Machinery has fallen into disrepair or is entirely obsolete. Under the arbitrary and destructive Nazi rule, virtually every possible enterprise was geared into the German war machine. Long-standing commercial ties, private institutions, banks, insurance companies, and shipping companies disappeared, through loss of capital, absorption through nationalization, or by simple destruction. In many countries, confidence in the local currency has been severely shaken. The breakdown of the business structure of Europe during the war was complete. Recovery has been seriously retarded by the fact that two years after the close of hostilities a peace settlement with Germany and Austria has not been agreed upon. But even given a more prompt solution of these difficult problems the rehabilitation of the economic structure of Europe quite evidently will require a much longer time and greater effort than had been foreseen.

There is a phase of this matter which is both interesting and serious. The farmer has always produced the foodstuffs to exchange with the city dweller for the other necessities of life. This division of labor is the basis of modern civilization. At the present time it is threatened with breakdown. The town and city industries are not producing adequate goods to exchange with the food producing farmer. Raw materials and fuel are in short supply. Machinery is lacking or worn out. The farmer or the peasant cannot find the goods for sale which he desires to purchase. So the sale of his farm produce for money which he cannot use seems to him an unprofitable transaction. He, therefore, has withdrawn many fields from crop cultivation and is using them for grazing. He feeds more grain to stock and finds for himself and his family an ample supply of food, however short he may be on clothing and the other ordinary gadgets of civilization. Meanwhile people in the cities are short of food and fuel. So the governments are forced to use their foreign money and credits to procure these necessities abroad. This process exhausts funds which are urgently needed for reconstruction. Thus a very serious situation is rapidly developing which bodes no good for the world. The modern system of the division of labor upon which the exchange of products is based is in danger of breaking down.

The truth of the matter is that Europe's requirements for the next three or four years of foreign food and other essential products—principally from America—are so much greater than her present ability to pay that she must have substantial additional help or face economic, social, and political deterioration of a very grave character.

The remedy lies in breaking the vicious circle and restoring the confidence of the European people in the economic future of their own countries and of Europe as a whole. The manufacturer and the farmer throughout wide areas must be able and willing to exchange their products for currencies the continuing value of which is not open to question.

Aside from the demoralizing effect on the world at large and the possibilities of disturbances arising as a result of the desperation of the people concerned, the consequences to the economy of the United States should be apparent to all. It is logical that the United States should do whatever it is able to do to assist in the return of normal economic health in the world, without which there can be no political stability and no assured peace. Our policy is directed not against any country or doctrine but against hunger, poverty, desperation and chaos. Its purpose should be the revival of a working economy in the world so as to permit the emergence of political and social conditions in which free institutions can exist. Such assistance, I am convinced, must not be on a piecemeal basis as various crises develop. Any assistance that this Government may render in the future should provide a cure rather than a mere palliative. Any government that is willing to assist in the task of recovery will find full co-operation, I am sure, on the part of the United States Government. Any government which maneuvers to block the recovery of other countries cannot expect help from us. Furthermore, governments, political parties, or groups which seek to perpetuate human misery in order to profit there from politically or otherwise will encounter the opposition of the United States.

It is already evident that, before the United States Government can proceed much further in its efforts to alleviate the situation and help start the European world on its way to recovery, there must be some agreement among the countries of Europe as to the requirements of the situation and the part those countries themselves will take in order to give proper effect to whatever action might be undertaken by this Government. It would be neither fitting nor efficacious for this Government to undertake to draw up unilaterally a program designed to place Europe on its feet economically. This is the business of the Europeans. The initiative, I think, must come from Europe. The role of this country should consist of friendly aid in the drafting of a European program and of later support of such a program so far as it may be practical for us to do so. The program should be a joint one, agreed to by a number of if not all European nations.

An essential part of any successful action on the part of the United States is an understanding on the part of the people of America of the character of the problem and the remedies to be applied. Political passion and prejudice should have no part. With foresight, and a willingness on the part of our people to face up to the vast responsibility which history has clearly placed upon our country, the difficulties I have outlined can and will be overcome.

John F. Kennedy

American University
June 10, 1963

Despite his short tenure as President before his assassination in November 1963, John F. Kennedy remains one of the most popular and revered men ever to sit in the White House. He also saw the United States and Soviet Union come to the brink of nuclear war during the Cuban missile crisis in October 1962. After that event and only months before his death, President Kennedy delivered this famous graduation speech at American University in Washington, D.C. These excerpts show a softening in Kennedy's hard-line demeanor with the Soviets and marks the first real appeal for détente between the two superpowers.

. . . Professor Woodrow Wilson once said that every man sent out from a university should be a man of his nation as well as a man of his time, and I am confident that the men and women who carry the honor of graduating from this institution will continue to give from their lives, from their talents, a high measure of public service and public support.

"There are few earthly things more beautiful than a university," wrote John Masefield in his tribute to English universities—and his words are equally true today. He did not refer to spires and towers, to campus greens and ivied walls. He admired the splendid beauty of the university, he said, because it was "a place where those who hate ignorance may strive to know, where those who perceive truth may strive to make others see."

I have, therefore, chosen this time and this place to discuss a topic on which ignorance too often abounds and the truth is too rarely perceived—yet it is the most important topic on earth: world peace.

What kind of peace do I mean? What kind of peace do we seek? Not a Pax Americana enforced on the world by American weapons of war. Not the peace of the grave or the security of the slave. I am talking about genuine peace, the kind of peace that makes life on earth worth living, the kind that enables men and nations to grow and to hope and to build a better life for their children—not merely peace for Americans but peace for all men and women—not merely peace in our time but peace for all time.

I speak of peace because of the new face of war. Total war makes no sense in an age when great powers can maintain large and relatively invulnerable nuclear forces and refuse to surrender without resort to those forces. It makes no sense in an age when a single nuclear weapon contains almost ten times the explosive force delivered by all the allied air forces in the Second World War. It makes no sense in an age when the deadly poisons produced by a nuclear exchange would be carried by wind and water and soil and seed to the far corners of the globe and to generations yet unborn.

Today the expenditure of billions of dollars every year on weapons acquired for the purpose of making sure we never need to use them is essential to keeping the peace. But surely the acquisition of such idle stockpiles—which can only destroy and never create—is not the only, much less the most efficient, means of assuring peace.

I speak of peace, therefore, as the necessary rational end of rational men. I realize that the pursuit of peace is not as dramatic as the pursuit of war—and frequently the words of the pursuer fall on deaf ears. But we have no more urgent task.

Some say that it is useless to speak of world peace or world law or world disarmament—and that it will be useless until the leaders of the Soviet Union adopt a more enlightened attitude. I hope they do. I believe we can help them do it. But I also believe that we must reexamine our own attitude— as individuals and as a Nation—for our attitude is as essential as theirs. And every graduate of this school, every thoughtful citizen who despairs of war and wishes to bring peace, should begin by looking inward—by examining his own attitude toward the possibilities of peace, toward the Soviet Union, toward the course of the cold war and toward freedom and peace here at home. . . .

. . . Today, should total war ever break out again—no matter how—our two countries would become the primary targets. It is an ironic but accurate fact that the two strongest powers are the two in the most danger of devastation. All we have built, all we have worked for, would be destroyed in the first twenty-four hours. And even in the cold war, which brings burdens and dangers to so many nations, including this Nation's closest allies—our two countries bear the heaviest burdens. For we are both devoting massive sums of money to weapons that could be better devoted to combating ignorance, poverty, and disease. We are both caught up in a vicious and dangerous cycle in which suspicion on one side breeds suspicion on the other, and new weapons beget counterweapons.

In short, both the United States and its allies, and the Soviet Union and its allies, have a mutually deep interest in a just and genuine peace and in halting the arms race. Agreements to this end are in the interests of the Soviet Union as well as ours—and even the most hostile nations can be relied upon to accept and keep those treaty obligations, and only those treaty obligations, which are in their own interest.

So, let us not be blind to our differences—but let us also

direct attention to our common interests and to the means by which those differences can be resolved. And if we cannot end now our differences, at least we can help make the world safe for diversity. For, in the final analysis, our most basic common link is that we all inhabit this small planet. We all breathe the same air. We all cherish our children's future. And we are all mortal. . . .

Martin Luther King, Jr.

Lincoln University
June 6, 1961

Few figures tower over modern American history as does the Reverend Martin Luther King, Jr. King used nonviolent marches and protests in the face of violent police resistance and brutality in such places as Montgomery, Birmingham, and Selma, Alabama, to help persuade the Kennedy and Johnson administrations to take active political steps to provide more equality for minorities in America. After his assassination in 1968 King became a symbol for the struggle against racial injustice everywhere. These excerpts from his commencement address at Lincoln University in 1961 touch on many of King's ideas of nonviolence and racial unity. The ending is almost identical to the end of his famous "I Have a Dream" speech in Washington, D.C., two years later.

... Today you bid farewell to the friendly security of this academic environment, a setting that will remain dear to you as long as the cords of memory shall lengthen. As you go out today to enter the clamorous highways of life, I should like to discuss with you some aspects of the American Dream. For in a real sense, America is essentially a dream, a dream as yet unfulfilled. It is a dream of a land where men of all races, of all nationalities and of all creeds can live together as brothers. The substance of the dream is expressed in these sublime words, words lifted to cosmic proportions: "We hold these truths to be self-evident, that all men are created equal, that they are endowed by their Creator with certain unalienable rights, that among these are life, liberty, and the pursuit of happiness." This is the dream.

One of the first things we notice in this dream is an amazing universalism. It does not say some men, but it says all men. It does not say all white men, but it says all men, which includes black men. It does not say all Gentiles, but it says all men, which includes Jews. It does not say all Protestants, but it says all men, which includes Catholics.

And there is another thing we see in this dream that ultimately distinguishes democracy and our form of government from all of the totalitarian regimes that emerge in history. It says that each individual has certain basic rights that are neither conferred by nor derived from the state. To discover where they came from it is necessary to move back behind the dim mist of eternity, for they are God-given. Very seldom if ever in the history of the world has a sociopolitical document expressed in such a profoundly eloquent and unequivocal language the dignity and the worth of human personality.

Ever since the Founding Fathers of our nation dreamed this noble dream, America has been something of a schizophrenic personality, tragically divided against herself. On the one hand we have proudly professed the principles of democracy, and on the other hand we have sadly practiced the very antithesis of those principles. Indeed slavery and segregation have been strange paradoxes in a nation founded on the principle that all men are created equal. This is what the Swedish sociologist, Gunnar Myrdal, referred to as the American dilemma.

But the shape of the world today does not permit us the luxury of an anemic democracy. The price America must pay for the continued exploitation of the Negro and other minority groups is the price of its own destruction. The hour is late; the clock of destiny is ticking out. It is trite, but urgently true, that if America is to remain a first-class nation she can no longer have second class citizens. Now, more than ever before, America is challenged to bring her noble dream into reality, and those who are working to implement the American dream are the true saviors of democracy. . . .

. . . I believe, more than ever before, in the power of non-violent resistance. It has a moral aspect tied to it. It makes it possible for the individual to secure moral ends through moral means. This has been one of the great debates of history. People have felt that it is impossible to achieve moral ends through moral means. And so a Machiavelli could come into being and so force a sort of duality within the moral structure of the universe. Even communism could come into being and say that anything justifies the end of a classless society—lying, deceit, hate, violence—anything. And this is where nonviolent resistance breaks with communism and with all those systems which argue that the end justifies the means, because we realize that the end is preexistent in the means. In the long run of history, destructive means cannot bring about constructive ends.

The practical aspect of nonviolent resistance is that it exposes the moral defenses of the opponent. Not only that, it somehow arouses his conscience at the same time, and it breaks down his morale. He has no answer for it. If he puts you in jail, that's all right; if he lets you out, that's all right too. If he beats you, you accept that; if he doesn't beat you—fine. And so you go on, leaving him with no answer. But if you use violence, he does have an answer. He has the state militia, he has police brutality. . . .

. . . As I have said in so many instances, it is not enough to struggle for the new society. We must make sure that we make the psychological adjustment required to live in that new society. This is true of white people, and it is true of Negro people. Psychological adjustment will save white people from going into the new age with old vestiges of prejudice and attitudes of white supremacy. It will save the Negro from seeking to substitute one form of tyranny for another.

I know sometimes we get discouraged and sometimes disappointed with the slow pace of things. At times we begin to talk about racial separation instead of racial integration, feeling that there is no other way out. My only answer is that the problem never will be solved by substituting one tyranny for another. Black supremacy is as dangerous as white supremacy, and God is not interested merely in the freedom of black men and brown men and yellow men. God is interested in the freedom of the whole human race and in the creation of a society where freedom of the whole human race and in the creation of a society where all men can live together as brothers, where every man will respect the dignity and the worth of human personality.

By following this method, we may also be able to teach our world something that it so desperately needs at this hour. In a day when Sputniks and Explorers are dashing through outer space, and guided ballistic missiles are carving highways of death through the stratosphere, no nation can win a war. The choice is no longer between violence and nonviolence; it is either nonviolence or nonexistence. Unless we find some alternative to war, we will destroy ourselves by the misuse of our own instruments. And so, with all of these attitudes and principles working together, I believe we will be able to make a contribution as men of good will to the ongoing structure of our society and toward the realization of the American dream. And so, as you go out today, I call upon you not to be detached spectators, but involved participants, in this great drama that is taking place in our nation and around the world.

Every academic discipline has its technical nomenclature, and modern psychology has a word that is used, probably more than any other. It is the word *maladjusted*. This word is the ringing cry of modern child psychology. Certainly all of us want to live a well-adjusted life in order to avoid the neurotic personality. But I say to you, there are certain things within our social order to which I am proud to be maladjusted and to which I call upon all men of good will to be maladjusted.

If you will allow the preacher in me to come out now, let me say to you that I never did intend to adjust to the evils of segregation and discrimination. I never did intend to adjust myself to religious bigotry. I never did intend to adjust myself to economic conditions that will take necessities from the many to give luxuries to the few. I never did intend to adjust myself to the madness of militarism, and the self-defeating effects of physical violence. And I call upon all men of good will to be maladjusted because it may well be that the salvation of our world lies in the hands of the maladjusted.

So let us be maladjusted, as maladjusted as the prophet Amos, who in the midst of the injustices in his day could cry out the words that echo across the centuries, "Let justice run down like the waters and righteousness like a mighty stream." Let us be as maladjusted as Abraham Lincoln, who had the vision to see that this nation could not exist half slave and half free. Let us be as maladjusted as Jesus of Nazareth, who could look into the eyes of the men and women of his generation and cry out, "Love your enemies. Bless them that curse you. Pray for them that despitefully use you."

I believe that it is through such maladjustment that we will be able to emerge from the bleak and desolate midnight of man's inhumanity to man into the bright and glittering daybreak of freedom and justice. That will be the day when all of God's children, black men and white men, Jews and Gentiles, Catholics and Protestants, will be able to join hands and sing in the words of the old Negro spiritual, "Free at last! Free at last! Thank God almighty, we are free at last!"

Lyndon B. Johnson

University of Michigan
May 22, 1964

*President Lyndon Johnson presided over one of the most
turbulent periods in American history in the mid to late 1960s.
He saw America tear itself apart over such questions as race
and the Vietnam War. But before these problems got out of
hand, Johnson enacted the series of sweeping domestic programs
known as the Great Society, the most ambitious social
legislation since the New Deal. Johnson envisioned a United
States where every person would have enough to eat, make a
livable wage, have the right to vote, and possess freedom from
persecution because of race, religion, or gender. In these
excerpts from his address at the University of Michigan,
Johnson first explained his ideas for this monumental program.*

... I have come today from the turmoil of your capital* to
the tranquillity of your campus to speak about the future of
your country.

The purpose of protecting the life of our Nation and preserving the liberty of our citizens is to pursue the happiness
of our people. Our success in that pursuit is the test of our
success as a Nation.

For a century we labored to settle and to subdue a continent. For half a century we called upon unbounded invention
and untiring industry to create an order of plenty for all of
our people.

*The capital Johnson refers to is Lansing, Michigan, where Johnson was greeted
by numerous protestors.

The challenge of the next half century is whether we have the wisdom to use that wealth to enrich and elevate our national life, and to advance the quality of our American civilization.

Your imagination, your initiative, and your indignation will determine whether we build a society where progress is the servant of our needs, or a society where old values and new visions are buried under unbridled growth. For in your time we have the opportunity to move not only toward the rich society and the powerful society, but upward to the Great Society.

The Great Society rests on abundance and liberty for all. It demands an end to poverty and racial injustice, to which we are totally committed in our time. But that is just the beginning.

The Great Society is a place where every child can find knowledge to enrich his mind and to enlarge his talents. It is a place where leisure is a welcome chance to build and reflect, not a feared cause of boredom and restlessness. It is a place where the city of man serves not only the needs of the body and the demands of commerce but the desire for beauty and the hunger for community.

It is a place where man can renew contact with nature. It is a place which honors creation for its own sake and for what it adds to the understanding of the race. It is a place where men are more concerned with the quality of their goals than the quantity of their goods.

But most of all, the Great Society is not a safe harbor, a resting place, a final objective, a finished work. It is a challenge constantly renewed, beckoning us toward a destiny where the meaning of our lives matches the marvelous products of our labor. . . .

. . . For better or for worse, your generation has been appointed by history to deal with those problems and to lead

America toward a new age. You have the chance never before afforded to any people in any age. You can help build a society where the demands of morality, and the needs of the spirit, can be realized in the life of the Nation.

So, will you join in the battle to give every citizen the full equality which God enjoins and the law requires, whatever his belief, or race, or the color of his skin?

Will you join in the battle to give every citizen an escape from the crushing weight of poverty?

Will you join in the battle to make it possible for all nations to live in enduring peace—as neighbors and not as mortal enemies?

Will you join in the battle to build the Great Society, to prove that our material progress is only the foundation on which we will build a richer life of mind and spirit?

There are those timid souls who say this battle cannot be won; that we are condemned to a soulless wealth. I do not agree. We have the power to shape the civilization that we want. But we need your will, your labor, your hearts, if we are to build that kind of society.

Those who came to this land sought to build more than just a new country. They sought a new world. So I have come here today to your campus to say that you can make their vision our reality. So let us from this moment begin our work so that in the future men will look back and say: It was then, after a long and weary way, that man turned the exploits of his genius to the full enrichment of his life.

Thank you. Good-bye.

Gloria Steinem

Smith College
May 30, 1971

Few women have left a more pronounced mark on their
generation than Gloria Steinem. A writer, journalist, and
political activist, Steinem became an eloquent voice for the
women's liberation movement of the 1970s. She remains a
strong role model for women to this day. A graduate of Smith
College, Steinem returned to give this landmark speech in
1971, the same year she helped found the National Women's
Political Caucus. It was also the same year she helped to
produce the first issue of Ms. *magazine.*

Friends and sisters, it's strange to come back to my own
college as a Commencement speaker; a little unsettling for
me. At our graduation ceremonies in 1956, when I sat before
this platform in cap and gown exactly as you sit before me
now, I had no ambitions nor even such dreams. Had I been
asked why not, I would not have known the answer. Because
speaking at Commencements is for other people, I might have
said, providing I took the question seriously at all. And in
my head, I would have pictured a man behind this podium,
a man probably old and definitely white. I had internalized,
without conscious thought and without formal instruction, the
racist and sexist values around me.

The non-white men and female human beings I had seen
in everyday life were usually dependent on acceptance by
white men in some overt or subtle way. I didn't look like the
ruling class, I was maybe even biologically and therefore im-

mutably inferior to it (unlike black men whom one insisted, if only intellectually, were just as good). And that was that.

Of course, no one asked me why my imagination couldn't stretch to Commencement speaking any more than they asked me why I didn't consider being a politician, a business executive, an engineer or even a writer. The dark fifties, I am afraid, were not brightened by much encouragement of women to be ambitious or autonomous—to dream unfeminine dreams. A more representative question was asked me by a vocational adviser when I brought up the subject of law school. "Why study three extra years and end up in the back room of some law firm doing research and typing," she said with great good sense, "when you can graduate from Smith College and do research and typing right away?"

Smith didn't invent the fifties any more than it invented the patriarchal and the racist system under which we continue to live. There have been many foresighted and courageous individuals who have worked to make this campus a more human place than the world around. It's changed since my day, for instance, there was not one black woman in the class, even though two-thirds of the applicants from the area around Washington, D.C., where I lived, were black. And when I asked a professor here why the black women had not been accepted, he explained that one had to accept only the strongest and the most outstanding, because it was going to be so hard for them in later life as there were not enough educated black men to go around. It is interesting, isn't it, how often racist arguments are used to support sexist standards and vice versa. In fact, there was not one black or non-white human being on the faculty or in the administration. Smith, a college with such feminist beginnings, was so lost to them that the administration offered, as a supposed inducement to prospective students, that the faculty was 75 percent male. The main excuse for educating us at all was that we would then educate our children. Indeed, the assumption was that we ourselves were children; creatures who were rarely encouraged to use in the real world all the knowledge being stuffed into our heads; creatures who were punished if we were not in our houses every week night by 10:15 p.m.

As you can see, much has changed. Through scholarship and recruitment programs, we white women are less ghetto-ized here now. Black women are joining us in growing num-bers and may even eventually represent at least the percentage that black Americans do in the overall population. Some res-titution is being made for the fact that here, as at most Amer-ican institutions, we have been studying white history, a history written for, by and about white men. There is now a Black Studies program and I understand that Smith is the only women's college to offer a Black Studies major. I am very proud of that.

We are even beginning to learn something about ourselves as women. I didn't know until last year, for instance, that the library had a fine collection of feminist literature. I understand that women *use* it now. There are a few women's studies courses, though still far short of the potential major and full department that Women's Studies should be. We are even beginning to recognize that women come here as adults, that if they chose not to enter college they would be voting for a president, working for a living, and becoming parents at the same age. Women students have many fewer rules now; perhaps soon they will be totally in charge of their own lives. College, after all, should be the beginning of adulthood, not an artificial prolongation of life as a child.

But there has been a larger change of consciousness in the last few years, a change in which Smith, as a women's college, should have been taking a lead. We have been discovering, in all areas of academic study and personal experience, that the so called masculine-feminine differences are largely societal, not biological; that those differences have application only to reproduction (supposing one chooses to reproduce), and that they have no meaning for education, job selection or life style. Indeed, that the myths of feminine inferiority have been used largely to suppress the talents and strengths of half the human race. . . .

I thought before I came here, that Smith, with its feminist beginnings, would be a free place where the repressive myths were being examined. The myth, for instance, that men need fulfilling work in addition to marriage and children, but that women, for some mysterious reason, do not. I had written a whole utopian speech about new social and political forms that would grow from this change. I thought we had understood the ultimate truth: that our inferior position all these hundreds of years had not been ordained by God or by biology, but was and is, in the purest sense, political.

For two days, I have been talking here to women students, and to women faculty, and to faculty wives. I have discovered that women here are still sometimes trapped into so-called feminine occupations. That the Vocational Office still routinely asks how many words per minute you can type, though the vocational offices at Amherst and Harvard do not. That the male supremacist teachings of Freud may be dead, I hope, but that some professors are still condescending to us out of minds that Freud and other male supremacists have formed. That the faculty is still 70 percent male and that some of the females on it have doubts about the way in which tenure is awarded or part-time female teachers are used. That encouragement of women's studies has often had to come from students or faculty wives and not from the College itself. That there is little emphasis on informing women of the real prejudice that they will meet, much less giving them philosophical and tactical tools to fight it. That there is still fear of so-called abnormal sexual behavior, whatever that means, whether it is too heterosexual or not heterosexual enough. That women students are still made to feel they have to worry more about combining marriage and a career than men do.

The sense of a wide range of alternatives for women has increased—but not enough. We are still being given skills and knowledge but not encouraged to use those skills and knowledge in the world as whole human beings.

So let me say to you some of the things that I wish so desperately someone had said to me. It would have saved me so much time and heartache.

As Virginia Woolf once said, bitterly, "Anonymous was a woman." It seems to me that both in high school and college, we generally started the study of history about the time of Charlemagne, right smack in a period of patriarchy and racism. In the earlier period, usually so graciously dismissed as pre-history, however, it turns out that we had such a thing as gynecocracy.

Indeed, for an earlier part of human history, more or less from perhaps 12,000 to 8,000 B.C., there's a lot of reason to believe that women were certainly equal and possibly superior; that women were worshiped *because* we had the children. We somehow have allowed ourselves to be talked into the notion that the bearing of children is an inferior function, but in those earlier days it was worshiped. Men's ceremonies imitated it. It was, in other words, a time of womb envy, not penis envy. And this continued until the discovery of paternity, a day I like to imagine as a big light bulb over somebody's head, and they're saying, "Oh, that's why!" Scholars, in fact, are now beginning to believe that women discovered paternity some years before they told anyone about it because they wanted to preserve their independence.

But, with the discovery of paternity, with the end of the notion that women bore fruit like trees until they were ripe, came a whole lot of institutions we will readily recognize.

The idea of ownership of property and of children, for instance, and the origin of marriage (which was really locking women up long enough to make sure who the father was), the subjugation of women . . . the notion that the state owns the body of a woman, a notion we still see in our abortion laws. As that grew, women became the first subjugated group; the group which all others were to follow in pattern. We were given the jobs to do that men did not want to do—that is still the definition of feminine work—and thus the pattern for other systems of unpaid or underpaid labor.

As other tribes and races were brought into this situation they were, as captured peoples, given the role of women. There has always been a very close parallel with all the second class groups. It is especially visible in this country with females and the largest second class group, which is blacks. I don't mean to equate the suffering. Gunnar Myrdal, who made this parallel thirty years ago, did not do that. Black men and women often lose their lives and white women more often lose their identities. But there are many parallels. We are both supposed to have smaller brains, passive natures, childlike natures, to be unable to govern ourselves—(God forbid we should try to govern a white male), to have special job skills (we are awfully good at detail work as long as it is poorly paid detail work—when it is brain surgery, we are suddenly not so good any more). These parallels are very important to understand because we have just barely begun to understand how deeply racist this society is . . . and must also admit how deeply male-dominated.

If we are to change this society in the deepest way, then all of us who have been marked for cheap labor, all of us must stand up together. We must resist those efforts that are made to turn us against each other. For instance, in many parts of the country there are political slates of the "outs"— white women, black women, black men, Puerto Ricans, Chicanos—who are forming slates together to try to break the hold of the white males on the state legislatures and on other political bodies.

We must realize something that we haven't up to now (and again I think there has been a kind of effort to keep us from realizing it), which is that women are sisters, that we have many of the same problems under patriarchy that the class divisions which men have made for themselves apply to men but not equally to us. The wife of a rich man is not usually a powerful person; she is often kept as an ornament and a child. She often comes to realize in the middle of the Movement that she may have more in common with her maid than she does with her husband. There are housewives who are suffering from a system designed to give the employer two for the price of one by paying the husband's salary and getting the full-time support services of the wives, too. Housewives and domestics are organizing together for a decent wage so that they don't have to end up begging or asking for alimony—which in our system is more like war reparations.

The cause is clearly shared with black and other women of color equally. Women who are poor are disproportionately from some minority group, and they suffer even more from the policies that deny them legal abortions, that send American women to their death and injury from botched abortions at a rate greater each year than American men die in Vietnam. Abortion is our number one health problem. . . .

I think black women are often an example to white women. They have had to be stronger and more courageous, and it is also true that black men tend to understand this desire for freedom and equality on the part of all women better than white men. As Bobby Seale says, "In a Panther house everybody does the dishes and everybody sweeps the floor, and everybody makes the revolutionary policy.' Because real manhood does not depend on the subjugation of anybody."

Women in prisons have special problems also. They are often given longer sentences for the same crimes that men commit, and they are often arrested in situations where men are not; for instance, prostitutes are arrested; their customers are not.

Addicts also have a special kind of problem. It is difficult to count the addict population in this country, but it is thought there are four times more women addicts than men. . . . Yet most of the treatment facilities are for men addicts. . . .

Beautiful women have their own kind of problem. It's a kind of you-get-the-liquor-we'll-get-the-girls psychology, which means that women are interchangeable moving parts; that a beautiful woman is much less likely to be taken seriously as a human being. And so-called unattractive women have fundamentally the same problem because all that they are, all that they try to do, is written off with the argument, "Well, they are only doing it because they can't get a man." So-called beautiful and so-called ugly women have a common cause in ending a system that values our looks more than our hands and hearts.

Older women are often more radical than young women. My own class, which came of age in the dark fifties and which is in the heart of its nesting period, is perhaps more conservative than the alumnae here who are forty or fifty years out. They have been through the system; they know. The women who are young sometimes say radical things but don't act upon them, because secretly they are preserving their ability to marry, to please men, to be dependent. Look to our older sisters who have done that and who know that that is not a human or possible solution, no matter how rich he is. We must have work of our own.

Students who are made to feel like half-people perhaps don't recognize that their situation is political. For example, one might consider this a typical political situation. You are going to a movie with a friend of yours, a women whom you like and respect, and a man from Amherst or elsewhere calls you. The man is four feet two, has terminal acne and no redeeming features of any kind, but you go—because you have been made to feel like half a person without a man.

Of course men and women need each other and love each other—and will continue to—but we don't need men *more* than they need us.

Love has almost been politicized out of existence. It really is only possible between equals. As soon in a relationship as you need him more than he needs you, a lot of other things begin to happen; a lot of Uncle Toming and giggling and pretending you don't know what you really know, and saying, "How clever of you to know it's Tuesday." A lot of men don't know whether they are loved for themselves or for their social identity and their wall-to-wall carpeting.

Sex is probably the same kind of situation. We have somehow arrived at a stage in which there is one subject and one object. Sex has almost become a kind of sado-masochistic relationship. Men have come to be so dependent on the idea of superiority that they think they cannot get along without it. I assure them that they can and that however used they may have got to submission, cooperation is better. . . .

Now you have become alumnae. I hope that you will place your own energies and any pressures at your disposal to making this College a women's college, and not a school for girls. Women need to know that there are all the choices of life available to them.

Couldn't there be a freshman orientation course (perhaps using some of our accomplished alumnae) that does something to enlarge the idea that somehow it's a job, or it's marriage, and there is nothing in between?

Couldn't we be concerned with the education of older women, and of poor women and of ways to get them into this institution, to give them its benefits, and to give us the benefit of their presence?

Couldn't we discuss in our political science courses and elsewhere the problem of the masculine mystique? How much that has influenced our foreign policy, how much of the reason that we are in Vietnam is because of the notion that masculinity depends upon the subjugation of other people?

Shouldn't we talk about the politics of marriage? In a real partnership, the wife's work is just as important and the husband is as likely to move to another city if his wife has great opportunity as she is to move for his. It is truly a partnerhsip only if both are responsible for the house and for the children. . . .

Shouldn't we discuss the politics of religion? Why is it that God always looks so exactly like the ruling class? As the position of the priesthood goes up, you find in all great religions, whether it is Hinduism or Catholicism, the position of women goes down. . . . I am happy to say that the situation is reversing itself, the position of the priesthood is going down and the position of women is going up. Radical nuns are taking over the pulpits from priests because we know that there is no reason why a woman should be a nun and a man a priest (or a woman a nurse and a man a doctor, or a woman a typist and a man the boss—perhaps a whole generation of us should fail to learn how to type). Protestant women are now voting in the church—a great revolution. Jewish women are rewriting the prayers, especially those in which Orthodox Jews thank God every morning for not having been born women.

Consider the politics of motherhood. We have seen that

the state regards us as a means of production. Isn't it interesting that motherhood becomes sacred, that the Madonna image is prevalent whenever the state needs workers and the state needs soldiers. Motherhood is not an instinct. . . . Sex in human beings has never been related to conception as it is in animals . . . so perhaps God, perhaps she, had something else in mind for us.

Obviously, it is important that we repeal all those obscene laws against abortion and that birth control be readily available. . . . Not everyone should be a parent any more than everyone with vocal cords should be an opera singer.

The politics of women's volunteerism is also something we should consider. After all, the idea of volunteering got started because men could not stand the challenge to their ego and their social status of a wage-earning wife. I suggest that we volunteer only to change the system, not to perpetuate it; that we stop the endless reading to invalids and working in hospitals that reduce the number of salaried jobs; that we volunteer only to force the government to pay for those things which it indeed has the money to pay for—if it would only start paying for life and not for death.

I think one of the questions before us now is the integration, the sexual integration of Smith College. I think perhaps we know in our hearts that we are not ready for it yet. Our heads are not together enough yet as women to be integrated with male students. I believe that this College has to turn into a real college for *all* women, that it has to become again a feminist institution, a radicalizing institution. . . .

For the next fifty years, until we get ourselves straightened out and men's identity depends less upon control, victory, and violence, women are going to be very valuable in positions of political influence. . . .

So, because I think that my presence here today is a small part, a very small part, of a change in the heads of students,

I am happy to be here. I am not happy to be one of five women Commencement speakers in the history of this College. That says a great deal, because it is the students that choose the speakers and we have usually chosen members of the ruling class. Fortunately, the recipients of honorary degrees, like the recipients of other Smith degrees, have always been women, and so we have been able to see, as you will see here today, many brave and courageous and talented women come before us. . . . I am honored to be here today as a beginning. Because I believe in honoring a female Commencement speaker, you are really honoring yourselves.

So perhaps if we live this revolution every day—which stretches all the way from thinking about calling ourselves Ms. to the demand for justice and equality in all areas of life—we will revolutionize the economy. . . . By standing up, by refusing to be cheap labor any more—whether it is in the kitchen or in the office or in the factory or on the campus— we will revolutionize this system. We will humanize it by a more compassionate distribution of goods, and services; and of human opportunity.

If we do, perhaps we have a chance for a third kind of period. After all, we may have had at least 5,000 years of the superiority of women. We have 5,000 years of patriarchy and racism. Perhaps we have a chance for 5,000 years of humanism.

Perhaps, if we really live this revolution every day, historians will look back at us and say that, for the first time, the human animal stopped dividing itself up according to visible difference—according to race, according to sex—and started to look for the real, the human potential inside.

Editors' Note

We would like to take this opportunity to thank the many people who contributed their time and effort to help make this project a reality.

First and foremost we'd like to thank our contributors. Every one of these very busy people—people who are flooded daily with requests for their time and effort—want to make a difference in this world. They care deeply about our future, and they recognized immediately an opportunity to speak directly to those in whose hands our future lies. We thank them for their graciousness.

Second, this project would not have been possible without the aid of the many, many personal assistants, researchers, and archivists who answered our queries, returned our phone calls, dug through mountains of material, and generally made themselves available to us. For their hard work we thank Julie Pampinella, Connie Croslin, Astrid Reid, Mary Finelli, Lucas Held, Jay German, Jennifer Helig, Gila Reinstein, Rina Romero, Jane Finalborgo, Kathleen Candy, and Vera Myers.

We would especially like to thank Cynthia Wang for her expert assistance in tracking down our contributors. We appreciate her taking so much time from her busy reporting schedule to provide us with this information and in the process save us a lot of valuable time and energy. Our deep thanks, Cynthia.

At William Morrow, we thank Paul Fedorko and Betty

Kelly for their support. We'd also like to thank Bradford Foltz, who did a superb job designing the jacket, Bernie Klein for the handsome interior design, and Pearl Hanig did a first-rate job with the copyediting. And being former editors ourselves, we recognize that every book needs to have a champion. We thank our editor, Ann Triestman, for being our champion. From the very first mention of this project, Ann brought the enthusiasm, the drive, and the expertise needed to make this book a reality. Thank you for your unwavering support and for doing a super job on the manuscript.

Sheldon Meyer, Leona Capeless, and Joellyn Ausanka taught us well at Oxford University Press, and we must thank them for caring enough to see that we learned our craft well. Anything we might do in the world of books, we owe to you. To us, you are family.

Which reminds us, of course, that we must thank our friends and families for bearing with us while we put our efforts into this book. Becky Trissler, for her support, inspiration, and love. Rick and Carol Johns for providing a "fortress of solitude" in nothern Illinois, and David and Kristina Albanese for their tireless support. We couldn't have done this, or much else, without you in our lives.

And of course we must thank the legendary George Plimpton for his involvement. We are honored that you took time out of your incredibly busy schedule to help write a wonderful introduction and to contribute a classic speech. Our sincere thanks.

—*Andrew Albanese*
New York

—*Brandon Trissler*
Antioch, Illinois